Dedicated to my dear wife Tayebeh

with enormous gratitude for her unceasing care

and support.

In Searching God

In Searching God

(Intellectuals of Cafe Naderi)

By

Bagher Mohama

In Searching God

4

Contents:

In Searching God

Introduction

In 2013, this book was published by AuthorHouse with the title of "Intellectuals of Café Naderi" and pen name of "Bagher Mohama". The title was taken from the nickname of a group of intellectuals who traditionally held their meetings in that café in Tehran. The pen name was part of my middle and first names. I was not at all happy with that publication. Now, I would like to revise it, edit and re-publish for the following reasons. When I began to write this book, the title I chose was "In Searching God". But later, some of the publishing agents advised me that in fact Intellectuals of café Naderi is a better title and more likely to attract the attention of book lovers. I think the main reason my proposed title was not approved by them was that, they judged me an unqualified person to talk about God. I would certainly admit this and agree with them if that was indeed what they meant. However, having accepted that reasoning I still prefer my first choice as it seems more fitting with the intention behind the writing of the book and therefore after revising and editing (with the help of a British friend), it will be re-published with that title. I must say that, although English is not my native language (and admittedly I am not fluent) I will not ask the professionals to edit as I want it be natural narrative and speech of a foreigner to this language, with all of its mistakes and shortcomings. Here I am not claiming a piece of literary art. As for the author's name, I chose the pen name simply because I wished the readers to concentrate on the subject of the book and, not on authority or merits of the author; to focus on <u>what</u> has been said, rather than <u>who</u> has said it. I must be honest and confess that not using the real name could also be due to my reluctance to show off or more likely the fear of being ridiculed, criticised and even prosecuted for reciting what those intellectuals had said about the religions and God. There were of course some serious political considerations too, to the extent that I began the narration by saying, "A few months before he sadly passed away, a dear friend of mine gave me his extensive notes….etc.", in order to pretend that what I was about to say, were not my views and beliefs but those of someone else. Now I feel I was too cautious and cowardly. I will of course, leave the first paragraph of the preface as it was; to preserve the originality of the book. As for the first publication, I realised too late that there were too many spelling or typing errors and missing words in the book but more significantly the design of the pages or paragraphing and usages of the punctuation marks were far from satisfactory. Of course, I must accept the responsibility for it rather than blaming the publisher. Indeed, I should have checked the final version of the book more carefully before it was passed to the publisher. I had wrongly assumed that, I only needed to check the final text; leaving the design of pages and chapters or correction of the spelling mistakes and spotting of the missing words to the publisher, before being printed. There will still be some errors of course, but I hope not as many as first publication. One more point ought to be explained here and that is about the intellectuals. There were quite a few groups of intellectuals who used to have their assemblies in that café and I was only involved with one of them. Therefore, this story and the opinions expressed in the book by no means refer to all of the intellectuals of Café Naderi or reflect their opinions. And probably, this is another reason why my first choice for the title of book is more appropriate and fair. Lastly, I will continue using the pen name for this edition too because my other book have already been published with that name. B. M.

Preface

A few months before he sadly passed away; a dear friend of mine gave me his extensive notes. These were about the fascinating account of struggle for freedom and also spiritual debates which he had with a group of intellectuals that spanned a quarter of century. He wished them to be structured, edited and published. I hereby fulfil my promise and do so in the way that I think he would have done himself if had the opportunity. Knowing him well for decades and having briefly discussed the outline of book with him (after I had gone through the notes) I am certain that he would have written the preface as follows and he would have both narrated it like a story and arranged the chapters as I have. However from here on; I would like him to be the narrator.

The story starts in my childhood with its innocent questions, thoughts and beliefs. Then it passes through the agonizing periods of doubts and uncertainties before coming to climax of political changes and my spiritual convictions. This is indeed the evolution of thoughts throughout years of my journey. As the intellectuals are from different schools of thoughts it is fascinating (as well as expected) to read; how strongly God's existence is denied in one chapter and defended in another or, how the falsehood and absurdity of religions is debated and ridiculed in one part and their reality, rationality and necessity deliberated in the other and indeed, how differently every one of us would contemplate over fundamental questions such as birth of the universe and emergence of life on earth. It is fair to claim that, in this book those essential questions are looked at from an entirely new angle and unique perspective. I do beg your patience in pursuing the story in order to appreciate it in its totality and no judging on any single chapter, please! The evolution of thoughts and beliefs will be manifested as one reads on.   I

strongly believe that, there has been no one in the entire history

of humans, who did not think about God regardless of belief or

disbelief in his existence.   There is a reason for this fact and I

will discuss it amongst the other points, later in the book. All

of us have made this journey and passed through the different

stages in our thoughts of God but perhaps some of us have

contemplated deeper and searched for the Truth more

persistently.   It is a bitter and tragic reality that throughout the

same history of man those in power had no time nor desire to

search for the answers or indeed care for the Truth, as they

were too busy using the religions in general and God

specifically; to terrorize the people, to rule them, and to use

and exploit them. Sadly, the powerful continue to do so (albeit

with the modern slogans, excuses and modern technology). In

the name of God they have robbed people with taxes, gifts, and

sacrifices. In the name of God they have committed atrocities,

murders, genocides, rapes, plunders and destructions beyond

belief. In the name of God and religions; tyrants have justified their crimes against humanity and it will continue to be the case generation after generation.

Like most of you, I too have lived with the mystery of God. I too have thought about the birth of universe and origin of life. Like everyone else, I have thought about mankind and the purpose of his emergence on this planet and I have longed for the Truth. Most likely you will find similarities in the passages of our journeys but I think outcome of contemplation and search could be different as well as the final conviction. This is indeed a strange journey in which we may use exactly the same routes but arrive at entirely different destinations or use totally different routes but arrive at exactly the same destination as everyone else. In this book I narrate passages of my spiritual journey alongside a group of intellectual associates with whom I had meetings and debates in a private room in Café Naderi. Here I give an account of the debates spanning more than a quarter of a century with highly talented intellectuals, philosophers, scientists, poets and artists but at the same time, I talk about my personal contemplation in searching for the Truth.   I also refer to the political highs and lows of the country whenever is relevant to my journey that, I present as a story. Of course, the question of God's existence is the centrepiece of all contemplations and debates narrated here.   Needless to say that; fundamental questions and ideas regarding the birth of the universe, the origin of life and especially emergence of humans are inseparable from the thoughts and debates about the existence of God.   So, in different chapters of this book, I have frequently referred to such questions and related theories and tried to explain my understanding and answer them. Repetition was unavoidable as, on the one hand the theories were constantly changing and on the other hand in different periods of the journey I had different views about them, based on debates with intellectuals and their influence on my thoughts and beliefs as well as my own readings and research. It is a fact that, the events we experience in our personal lives, including social and political ones, shape our perception and beliefs of the spiritual and materialistic worlds and, such experiences make us what we are. To this end I have briefly referred to my political involvements and activities in a book which is primarily about the "spiritual evolution" of those from whom I quote, using their words from my notes and memory. Truly, I have no claim at all to be a philosopher, researcher, theoretician or authority in any religion or indeed anything else for that matter. But having said so, the fact that on the other side of debates, they were all distinguished thinkers and scientists; it makes the report worth reading. Indeed I'm only an ordinary member of the society, who simply could not resist the temptation of taking the readers through some of the passages of this fascinating journey; by writing a book about it and about his dreams and hopes for the humans. B.M.

Chapter 1

The initial conviction

I was an eleven-year-old boy when for the first time in my life I seriously thought about God. It happened well over half a century ago when we had just arrived in the noisy city of Tehran; leaving behind all that we had in a small town of Azerbaijan, and I was in bed on top of the roof of a house; fascinated with the beauty and elegance of the heavens.

My father, who was a landowner and also a merchant, had lost his empire and had no choice but to leave that town with his wife and children taking with them few basic belongings and a small sum of money. The collapse of his empire had happened gradually in two separate periods. The first phase occurred during the Bolshevik revolution of Russia, when his trade with that country was disrupted with heavy losses.

Many years later, I remember playing with Russian currency (Manat - Ruble) which was left in a big trunk. I liked to cut their beautiful pictures and stick them into my notebook. The next phase happened during the Second World War when Azerbaijan was briefly separated from the motherland and ruled by the communist party of Azerbaijan during which; my father's lands in several villages were confiscated and given to the peasants. There was of course, the factor of bitter rivalry amongst the relatives too that accelerated the total collapse of the empire.

Until that age, I had seen nothing except for our own or relatives' houses, some shops and few cars and carriages in the town. But now I had travelled six hundred kilometres by bus and had seen many buildings, villages, towns and cities. I had met numerous people of different appearance, costume and language on the way to the capital. In those days the roads were not at all good and travelling was not easy. Our journey took more than twenty four hours to complete, with several minor accidents, breakdowns and long stoppages. And I had the opportunity to see gigantic mountains, tunnels, valleys at close quarters as well as the forest, river and sea from far distances before the completion of our journey. For the first time in my life I had eaten and drunk in a restaurant or tearoom sitting close to strangers and curiously watching their behaviours which were entirely different from those I had been brought up with. I was youngest of the travellers and during the journey everyone was expecting me to fall sleep but I hardly did. The things that I was observing were too exciting to be able to sleep. It seemed as if I had borrowed a pair of extra eyes and was looking everywhere and at everything; with striking avidity and hunger. Indeed, I was overwhelmed by the breath-taking beauties of nature and I was amazed to find out how big was the world. When we finally entered the capital it was night and the city was full of lights, many small and big cars, buses, trucks and people. Most of the people we met spoke Persian and it was difficult for me to understand them. My mother language was Azeri and although my education had begun in Persian (Farsi) and, I ought to have been familiar with the language, I could not follow their accent easily. Our vehicle eventually stopped at a dirty bus station and from there, we were taken to a small house by minicab through the crowded streets; maddened by the deafening noises of the cars and drowned in dazzling lights. Whatever I saw was new to me; so puzzling and so confusing. The events and changes over the last couple of days were well beyond the capacity of my understanding. I had of course, barely realised that my father was no longer a rich man and we had to sell everything we had including the house with all the furniture in it. Having been brought up in an aristocratic family and having lived in a big house with huge gardens, swimming pool and having a bedroom of my own, I had now entered into a small rented house with hardly any garden and only three bedrooms and one reception for my parents, their six children and our eldest brother with his wife and three children. In fact having fled to the capital before us, he had rented the house for his own family and we had now temporarily joined them with the intention of finding a suitable accommodation for us in due course.

*

It was summer time and Tehran is usually hot during this season. Interestingly, during the day rooms inside, were usually cool but at night, when the weather outside would change to fresh and mild, inside the rooms could be too hot and stuffy to tolerate.   In those days most of such houses did not have air conditioning and traditionally people slept on purposely made wooden beds, under the sky in the gardens, or on top of the flat roofs of the houses.   I was excited with my first experience of such an interesting way of escaping the heat and having a pleasant sleep under the beautiful stars. Exhausted from the journey and puzzled by the diversity of the things that I had seen; I was in bed on the roof of this house (alongside my siblings and nephews) hoping to have a nice and peaceful sleep. The house was in a very poor area of the city and the neighbours' roofs were full of equally poor people who were making a lot of noise, arguing about different things.

On our side of the roof everyone was talking and joking except me. In my silence I was eagerly listening to their conversations, while staring at the sky that was covered by several thousands of the shiny stars. The beauty of the heavens was beyond any dispute and my fascination with its elegance and splendour beyond description. I was never so close to the sky and those shiny stars. On top of the roof (lying in bed on my back) I was completely taken over by this majestic view and I barely could see anything else. Numerous stars surrounded me and the magnificent sky was like a dome above the roof. It seemed that the stars were dragging me towards the heavens and it appeared that in a childish way somehow I had perceived the seriousness of life and had a vague comprehension or feeling of its mysterious profoundness.   Strangely, I felt a kind of loneliness amongst the crowd and sadness filled my heart.   Huge changes in our circumstances, the amazing trip that I had and things that I had seen, certainly had matured me.   It seemed that I had grown up a good few years in just a few days.   I was not thinking like a child anymore and was asking serious questions of myself.   My father, who was a devoted religious man, had already taught me that God created everyone and everything in the world.   He is everywhere all the time and sees all of us and knows precisely what we do and what we think.   He had also told me that there is only one God and he is the most compassionate.   God loves and protects us from all the dangers but he will also punish us if we make any mistakes or do anything wrong.   I had heard too many terrifying stories about the wrath of God and terrible punishments he had inflicted upon the people.   I had already heard and learned many things about God but this was the first time that I had the chance to appreciate his greatness.   How clever he must be (I said to myself), to create such a huge world with so many fascinating things in it including all those stars which had captured my imaginations. Fixing my eyes on those stars I was wondering how he has made them so shiny and why they don't fall down.

Older people on the roof were telling me that, the stars are much bigger than what we see and some of them are even bigger than where we live.   My brother showed me the big and small bears. He also tried to show and explain Milky Way and, how the travellers in the deserts use these signs to find their way.   They said that each one of us has a star and I immediately chose one for myself close to the Greater bear so that I would not lose it.   Every night I watched the sky for hours and I thought about the nature of twinkling stars, about the moon, the breath-taking beauty of the heavens and the grandeurs of creation and creator. I thought about the God and his power for a long time before I fell asleep every single night of that memorable summer. I saw a star that moved very fast, drew a shiny line in the sky and disappeared. I was told that it happens when the owner of star dies. They actually stressed the point that when we die our star dies too. I was deeply saddened by such information and kept watching my own star anxiously; worrying that it might disappear any time and I wept when I could not find it easily, fearing that I was about to die.

*

The more I thought about the shiny stars the more I comprehended how great God must be and indeed how big and fascinating is the world. Of course, at that time I had no idea that what I had seen until then was merely a tiny part of a huge country and that huge country was a very small piece of Planet Earth. I did not know that Earth is only a small planet amongst our solar system and the entire solar system itself with sun, earth, moon, eight other planets and their moons is only a fraction of our Galaxy and this Galaxy is one of the billions of the other Galaxies and truly, some of them are much bigger than ours. I had no idea that the Planet Earth, in comparison with the entire universe, is not even a dot let alone the small part of the country that I had seen and had assumed to be the whole world. I had no clear understanding of the universe and in my mind world meant everything that God has created. I did not know that as a matter of fact stars die and the new ones are born regularly and the shiny things that moved in the sky and disappeared were not stars. Interestingly, the lack of such information and knowledge made no difference at all because, I was sufficiently impressed with the size of the world anyway and was overwhelmed by ingeniousness of God and his unquestionable greatness and power. As a matter of fact, when I seriously think about the extent of my fascination and appreciation of God's greatness at that age and about the magnitude of their effect on my mind, I cannot envisage how any extra information or anything else for that matter; would have added to the intensity of my feelings. Even if such information and knowledge were available, and even if I could have understood them. Of course, it could have helped if I had known the things which looked like disappearing stars were in fact meteors not real stars and these so called shooting stars had nothing to do with stars, nor death of anybody. Of course, it could have been a consolation on those worrying nights, when I could not find my star and felt so miserable.

Until that age my conviction was that "God" exists and he created everything in the world **just because my father had told me so**. But now, I had appreciated and accepted that he was indeed great, most clever and very powerful. I thought that the creation of stars must be considered as his masterpiece. I must say that I was not comfortable with the information about God's punishment and the fact that, he is everywhere and constantly watching me to punish as soon as I made a mistake or did something wrong.   It is true to say that I did not love God but I respected and admired him a great deal for his most clever and ingenious way of creating not only those beautiful shiny stars but also the entire world.   More than anything else I was deeply touched and hugely impressed by God's exceptional qualities of Omnipotence, Omnipresence and Omniscience. At that stage I feared him more than anyone and anything else in the world and, such fear overshadowed all of the fascinations that I had for his qualities.   Fear of God is a subject that I will return to later on.

Chapter 2

Doubts

After summer, I started school and, although to begin with I had a lot of problems communicating with other children and both at school and the street where we had rented a house, I was bullied and teased, but I had no difficulty learning the lessons nor in doing my school or homework. In those days, the pupil who had the best scores in exams was called the Prime Student.   After the first semester they introduced me as such and this instantly put an end to all the bullying or teasing and at the same time many so called friends surrounded me. Obviously, it was not true friendship and they just needed me to help them to finishing their school work. However, in spite of having quite a few newly acquired friends, I never liked to stay out after the school (to play with them) or, play with the neighbours' children in the street. Of course, my parents would not have approved it either, even if I wanted to. So I had plenty of free time to utilise and somehow the idle gaps had to be filled.

There is no doubt that, I liked the school very much and truly appreciated the opportunities to learn but things, which were taught there didn't satisfy me and I longed for something a bit different without actually knowing what. So, having lots of spare time and with the desire to know more, I grew fond of reading extracurricular books that to begin with were children's books but after a couple of years I began to read more serious ones. For years, I spent all my pocket money buying or borrowing books and I developed a strange habit of starting with one author and finishing all his or her work, as much as I could find of course, before switching to another author. This habit provided opportunity to appreciate the thoughts and ideologies of each writer better. Soon, I became very interested in the books on philosophy, religions and history of religions and before I entered Medical School, I had read too many books and had totally confused myself. The more I read philosophical and religious books, the more I was confused and in fact, doubted God's existence. Sometimes I wished that I had never read philosophical or religious books in the first place. It may sound ridiculous of course but I must say that, whenever I carefully read and seriously contemplated on the thoughts and reasoning of a philosopher (as described in his book) whether he was trying to prove God's existence or reject it I thought that, he was absolutely right and no thinker could ever put any argument against his reasoning or thoughts. But when I read another philosopher's book that disagreed with the first one, I thought he was right too! I suppose with my immature and untrained brain, this ridiculous and confused mentality although not unexpected but was very distressing indeed. I am afraid, religious books and books regarding the history of religions that I had hoped would clarify matters did not help at all.

15

Because it seemed to me that there was much rubbish in them and indeed they contained numerous ludicrously disgraceful stories. The content of some ancient scriptures and so-called sacred books seemed to me more like cheap fiction; full of dirty plots, robberies and rape or lustful behaviours and unbelievable crimes. And apparently most of them were committed by gods, prophets or kings of the religions related to these books. Most of the stories, particularly those related to the sexual activities of ancient prophets and priests are not appropriate to quote in this book. The inconsistency in matters attributed to God was also confusing. Many conflicting accounts of the events in relation to God were given in the scriptures and different names and images were attached to him. To clarify this point, I bring a few less embarrassing examples of what had troubled me, had caused doubts and confusion and consequently had raised many questions in my mind. Is it possible to see God, talk to him and describe his form? Well, Jesus says no; "No man has seen God at any time." (John 1:18) The Quran says no too. But Jacob says yes: "I have seen God face to face and my life has been preserved." (Genesis 32:30).   And I had read in several books that prophet Moses saw and talked to God on many occasions.   Many other ancient prophets such as: Isaiah, Elijah, Ezekiel, Daniel, Habakkuk, Amos and Enoch had also claimed to have seen God and walked and talked with him.   Even Jesus, who people had seen and talked to for years, later on claimed to be God himself.   A God that was seen; lived with and talked to. So I asked myself could we see God or not? Could we define his image and voice?   Was Jesus a man, son of God or God himself? I am afraid religious books did not clarify any of my queries and the interpretations of those who attempted to explain and justify the claims or stories and events that are described in those scriptures could not convince me either. The image and voice of God had been clearly described in the books attributed to ancient prophets and religious leaders.   I was grieved to note that some of the descriptions were more suitable for a description of a prehistoric wild beast than God. I could not believe my eyes as I read through these books and imagined the horrible images of God that they presented. The number of the gods referred to in these books was confusing too. I had been taught and, until then had believed that, there could not be more than one God and we could not see him. So, I was bewildered, with the contents of some of the sacred books and, could not understand what they portrayed.

The other point I questioned was the ownership of God. I had been taught that he created everything and everyone and belongs to all human beings. So I wondered why the ancient books refer to him as God of Israel or God of the Bible (even though it seems that they believed in one God). What does it mean then? I asked. Does it mean that the rest of the people do not need or deserve to have God? Or, perhaps they were trying to suggest that every nation or religion should have its own one God. I thought the latter must be what they really meant which explains why their personal God should merely love one group of the people and without mercy wipe out several other nations in their favour as described in ancient books. Regarding the name, my understanding was that many different names were given to God and this was not just due to the difference in language used (which is expected) but these books were actually referring to a different God in different periods of the time with their own specific personalities, shapes and voices. I was indeed horrified to note some of the religious books had implied that God had parents, siblings and children and was dividing his land and wealth amongst them. They had even identified a dwelling place for the Most High and had indicated that, God killed countless people, only because they had dared to touch his dwelling. I could not digest or tolerate this nonsense any more.

There were so many preposterous and shameful stories and ludicrous attributions to God that, I thought those who had written those books (consciously or unconsciously), not only mocked God and made a fool of him but they also, had insulted, humiliated and dragged the "Most High" down to a very low level and had made him untrustworthy.

The purpose of this book of course, is to take the reader through some of the passages of my journey. It is not a research book but I refer to more specific examples, to justify my doubts at the start of the quest and highlight the intensity of my confusion which was indeed agonisingly distressing. As a young person I could not understand why God who is omnipotent; needed to stay on top of a mountain for forty days and nights, alongside prophet Moses in order to inscribe his guidance on a stone.   I thought even if it was really necessary for him to inscribe it on stone, he could have done it in a fraction of a second without any assistance or instrument. I did not believe my eyes when I read that omnipotent God wrestled with his prophet throughout a night and worse still he was not victorious after all, so in his rage broke Prophet Jacob's hip! To me, this story that had been repeated in many scriptures and other books portrayed the God as an ordinary young man who wished to wrestle just for the fun of it and, that was not the God I had been told about. I went on to read and was further educated "That is why to this day Israelites do not eat thigh sinew which is at the hip socket." (Genesis 32:33).When I read the following example, I honestly thought that it was only a tasteless and silly joke that God was so interested in foreskin of the male genitalia that demanded his prophet Abraham to circumcise himself and all male members of the family as a sign of the covenant. And he was running after Moses (or was it Abraham?) in a desert to kill him, when God found out or assumed that the prophet had not yet circumcised himself. But unfortunately, this was not joke and the story had been referred to in several sacred books. "You must circumcise the flesh of your foreskin and that will be the sign of the covenant between me and you. As soon as he is eight days old, every one of your males generation after generation ought to be circumcised."(Genesis, 17:11-14). I was of course, aware of the controversy regarding male circumcision as some believe it is a good practice some do not, but I could not imagine God would choose such a thing to seal the covenant. Sadly there were more examples. Like an ordinary person God liked certain foods and smells, "God loves the smell of a burnt ram." (Exodus, 29:18). He had eaten and drunk as guest of Prophet Abraham, "God had griddle cakes, butter, milk and veal prepared by Abraham's wife Sarai." (Genesis.18:8). And he was so exhausted that needed a full day of rest, after heavy work of creation for few days, "And God blessed the seventh day and sanctified it because in it he had rested from all his work which God created and made." (Genesis. 2:2-3).

The other thing that put me off and raised questions in my mind was the tyranny, bloodshed, rape, plunder, prosecution, burning and destruction described in sacred books. According to these books, most of the mass murders, genocides and the cruelties were done either by the order of God or at his direct action. I couldn't imagine how such unbelievable crimes (as described in these sacred books), could be on God's order or his direct action. Was it really God who committed such atrocities and crimes (I asked myself as I read the books) or was it tyrant kings and priests who did it in his name? I thought the latter ought to be the case but I was disappointed and disgusted to see that the scriptures had implied otherwise. There were many worse examples in the history books and scriptures that raised this question. Should I disregard religious books (especially the ancient scriptures) and accept God's existence outside the religions? Or, should I totally forget about him if he is really the kind of entity that scriptures have described; so foolish, so untrustworthy and so cruel?

My uncertainties about the existence of God began to increase quite quickly and I could no longer persuade myself to respect the sacred books representation of God. Doubts were agonising and uncertainties distressful and perplexing. To begin, with the doubts had been triggered by the powerful arguments and reasoning of the philosophers who did not believe in God, but later, the religious books with utterly absurd, disgraceful and humiliating stories about God had reinforced it. Of course, reading the research books written by atheists and infidels had a huge role too. But I honestly felt much more let down, troubled, confused and disappointed; after reading the books of theists, than studying the ones which were written by nonbelievers. Gradually, uncertainties and doubts in my mind amplified and intensified further and further to the extent that in the meetings with my intellectual friends I felt rather embarrassed as if the believing in God was a disgraceful and humiliating conviction at our level of the intellect? At this stage of journey, although there were strong doubts in my mind I had not yet rejected God. Something or more likely someone deep inside me was holding me back,

24

which seemed to be part of my own self. This feeling was not yet sufficiently clear for me to recognize and acknowledge its, his or her existence within me.

In Searching God

Chapter 3

Does God exist?

Towards the end of my secondary school I gradually became involved in political activities against the dictatorship of the king (known as the Shah in the west) and in the process of that, I made quite a few new friends all of whom were famous intellectuals of the time. I managed to make my way into their circle; a circle that grew very fast and became the most imperative centre of intellectuals and political activities in the country for at least a quarter of century, if not more. When I made closer acquaintance and joined their circle, I had already entered Medical School and a different life had begun for me both in the politics and education. The newly acquainted intellectual friends, who were delighted with my doubts and desire to find the answers to my queries, promised to rescue me from a distressing situation; the agony of uncertainties and doubts. They hoped all being well, that after a short period of time, I would be converted to a proper and respectful atheist, exactly like themselves! "It is a pleasure to help you." they said. My relationship and discussions with those intellectuals rapidly increased and I met them at least once a week. They were doctors, scientists, lawyers, thinkers, poets, writers and different types of artists and all; very bright, highly educated and in their own words were committed atheists and infidels. In those days being a nonbeliever or anti religion was fashionable for so-called educated people and it was an essential requirement for entering to the societies of the intellectuals. I was much younger than them and I had not yet rejected God and so, by definition I was not qualified to be in their presence but they were happy for me to mix with them because they assumed my doubts were very strong and most likely I was ready to admit atheism. They believed that awakening of the lost people (like me!) and freeing them from the dangers brought by the restrictive and indeed regressive forces of religions and theism was part of their intellectual responsibilities and duties. And I must admit they took their task seriously. They had of course allocated another duty for themselves and that was getting rid of dictatorship of Shah and bringing freedom and democracy to the people of our country. Political activities of this extremely influential group of the intellectuals were restricted to the delivering speeches and publishing of articles, poems and books in order to educate the people of their rights, to wake them up, mobilise and prepare them for revolution. They never joined the working class, in their street demonstrations, protests, strikes and armed struggles against the Shah's regime. This of course changed later in struggle, as I will describe in its place. Having said so many intellectuals were already imprisoned and some were under house arrest. They used to meet in a private room of a café called Café Naderi to eat, drink and discuss or more appropriately I must say to argue about different subjects for hours. They were known as the

Loquacious Intellectuals of Café Naderi and were often ridiculed by the working class for their empty talks and for never joining the uprisings in person.

*

In many meetings we debated religion, God and of course, politics. They were against any type of religion and wished to deal with them first, before talking about God. The intellectuals sought to convince me that even the so called monotheistic higher religions are neither logical proof for the existence of God nor; their foundation, establishment and doctrines, had anything to do with God, if one believes that he exists in the first place. Their plan and tactic was to briefly describe each religion and prove their absurdity and falsehoods, as well as the failure of their founders, to demonstrate any rational and acceptable link, between such religious establishments and the One True Universal God. Therefore, based on such a strategy they began demolishing the religions by referring to the history of every religion and presenting a brief summary of their doctrines. Obviously, neither had they any intention in those days to discuss the religions in details nor do I mean to do so, in this book. I will only give a narrative account of our meetings, discussions and their reasoning from surviving notes and from memory; to illustrate a major but very sad passage of my spiritual journey. Occasionally, I will also refer to ups and downs of the political activities that we had together, and to the social situation of country in those days.

There have been various religions in the history of man, which we did not intend to discuss all as most of them were not worth mentioning nor spending time. We decided to disregard the idolatry of primitive people and basic polytheism of the ancient nations such as Greeks, Romans and Egyptians so that we did not waste our time. We did not think that worshiping of human gods and later on their various substitutes and worshiping statues and sacred animals or, worshipping and praying for the forces in nature; were worth deliberating and we did not regard their religions as truly theistic ones anyway. At first intellectuals thought that they could probably pass ancient religions of India and neighbouring states too beside the other polytheistic beliefs but then they decided to have a brief discussion about the Hinduism and Brahmanism anyway, merely for the philosophical and spiritual aspect of their teachings and practices which make them rather different from the other polytheistic religions. Alongside it of course, we also referred to the subjects such as asceticism, recluses and many other similar categories.

*

"The problem is that," began the first assassin of the religions, as they were named so, "there are too many branches, divisions, subdivisions and schools in the ancient religions that, it is virtually impossible to conduct a logical

32

debate about them or present a clear description of them. However, in their own sacred books, teachings and practices, (depending on which division and school you are looking at) one could find obvious suggestions for the polytheism as well as monotheism, pantheism and even atheism. Therefore, right from start it doesn't seem that you will be able to find your (one universal God) in these religions." said the speaker. "In fact, not only polytheism is manifest in most divisions of Brahmanism and Hinduism but also, worshiping statutes and paintings or offering food, gifts and sacrifices to gods and the bizarre rituals and ceremonies that they have adopted; makes them indistinguishable from the religions of idolaters. But of course, the doctrine of self-development comes to their rescue from such likeness." added the infidel reluctantly, and continued to demolish further, "Some schools might object to what I say and claim monotheism but the fact is that they all worship the ancient Vedic gods such as Indra, Agni, Vayu, Surya, Varuna, Vishnu, Shiva and the most high amongst them

Brahma plus the rest of 33 or 34 gods in their list. Apart from these gods they also believe in a much bigger god called Brahman which is different from the Brahma. I believe you are confused by now." said the speaker laughingly and seemed rather amused. At this point one of the intellectuals interrupted him by saying, "Polytheism of Hindus is basically Pantheism in which various deities are regarded as aspects of the one." "But I reckon," said one of the intellectuals who did not participate in the debates seriously but from time to time, interrupted the speaker with a joke and comment, "Brahman is their main god and the rest of them are juniors or assistants and, Brahma acting as head of the juniors." The speaker ignored the joker's bright idea and continued, "Their teaching and practices may or may not lead to the self-development and awakening as they wish but, the very fact is that not only there is no mention of your one universal God but, even the Vedic gods are lost in the excessive austerities, asceticism and practices of the rituals." He paused and seemed unhappy with his own description of a religion that has hundreds of millions of believers but he did not give up. "By the way," he continued, "each person worships one of the deities as his personal god which is a matter of individual preference." He then added with obvious sarcasm, "Well, I suppose it is quite luxurious to have your personal god at home so that you could get hold of it whenever you need, don't you agree?" The intellectuals observed that like any other religion, in this one too the priests essentially seek their own interests and glories in numerous ways including making the blind obedience of them; an important requirement if believers dream of enlightenment and Nirvana. "The Brahmin priests regard themselves from higher social classes" said the speaker, "and claim to be the chosen people, descended from twelve noble tribes." Exactly like the Israelites, who also claim to be the chosen nation and descendants of 12 tribes? Interesting similarity, isn't it?" Remarked our attentive joker but once again the speaker continued his line with no comment on joker's point.

35

"Brahmin priests regard themselves as the purest beings that have the highest knowledge of Veda, (the most ancient sacred writings) and are the only persons who could and should teach the others and like all other religions the priests claim to possess special knowledge that is denied to the commoners. Brahmin priests claim that they are created from Brahma's head and they are in fact God incarnates and therefore, obeying and serving them is equal to serving the God." He then while searching the effects of his recital on me asked, "Can you now see the real purpose behind making these religions?"

Like most of the religions, it appeared to us that, Hinduism and Brahmanism had been prompted by the political, social and economic considerations and predominantly for the purpose of protecting the interests of upper class than anything else. But of course, over the decades certain spiritual, moral and philosophical materials were added by the philosophers and scholars. "However," summed up our nonbeliever, "not

36

only we have failed to find your universal God in this religion but also, there is not a single logical reason to accept that God's prophet founded it and it appears no one knows who started it anyway.   The reality is that these are merely the ideologies and doctrines which were put forward by thinkers or those in power for whatever good or evil purposes they might have had in their minds. Obviously, subsequently the idea evolved and became a religion attracting many believers."   I replied to the intellectuals and made it clear that I was not expecting them to find God for me in these religions.   I told them that I had already studied the ancient religions of India and neighbouring nations and I was fully aware of absence of God in them or if there is any mention of him it was of secondary significance.   I also declared to my intellectual friends that neither would I accept the idea of rebirth (as one of their principals), nor subject of incarnation and reincarnation as a whole in this religion or any others.   They were very pleased to hear this and the speaker happily jumped to the conclusion.

"If you are accepting that there is no sign of God in any one of the religions" he said, "we could forget about the rest and sort out mystery of your God; separately and unrelated to these absurdities." That was not what I had meant and so they continued with their purpose of dismissing the religions first.

*

To my astonishment; for Zoroastrianism the religion of Persians before Islam, the intellectuals did not show much hostility. "About 600 BC Zoroaster brought this religion," said one of the intellectuals, "although some people believe Zoroastrianism is older that. However he was against the polytheistic belief within the country and so, introduced Ahura Mazda as the only uncreated God and, the only one who created the entire universe. He also believed that there is constant battle between Ahura Mazda, representing the good forces, and Ahriman or the devil, representing the bad forces, a battle between light and dark. He presented his gospel of monotheism in simple methods adapted to understanding of the people that he taught as it was impossible to deliver his teaching with its philosophical matters in any other way".

"By the way," said one of the intellectuals, "centuries later Jesus did exactly the same by using parables to convey his moral and spiritual ideas to people." The main speaker continued with his account, "Zoroaster was perhaps the first thinker who identified the darkness and lightness within the human being and outside world. He was certainly one of the first to define the Heaven as the best state of mind and Hell as the worst state. He taught righteousness; right thinking or purity of the mind, right speaking (good words), right conduct and resistance of oppressors. He also produced explicit hygienic laws and firmly believed that, the health and purity of one's body, prepares one for the purity of mind and soul. He instructed a daily bath in the mornings and careful hand washing before prayers and meals."

Here, the speaker paused and hesitated for longer than expected and appeared that he was trying to find a way out of his sympathetic description of this religion. "Okay, this all sounds very well," Said he after that break, "but it doesn't prove anything specific. All it shows is that, Zoroaster was a philosopher and reformer who introduced a way of life in order to establish better human society and suggested that there is only one God as the creator." This didn't help his confused mind and he still seemed uncertain how to end that debate and therefore, he looked at the others to see, whether one of them comes to his rescue. "Having said so," he decided to carry on regardless, "it is interesting to note that, Zoroaster believed Ahriman was God too, of course he meant the bad one. If that was the case then we have a problem with his monotheism and probably he was a dualist."

"In my humble view it is much better than polytheism." said the funny infidel. But at this point one of the intellectuals asked the speaker's permission to offer further information about dualism and said, "The real dualist was Mani (a Persian) who established a dualistic religion (Manichaeism) in the third century which spread rapidly to Africa and Europe, mainly to the Roman Empire and finally died out in sixth century." "Zoroaster prophesised," continued main narrator after that information, "that in future more prophets like him would come, to lead the humanity onwards until the Day of Judgment. But we can neither find a single reason to believe that, God sent Zoroaster as his prophet, nor that the foundation of Zoroastrianism confirms God's existence." The Intellectuals acknowledged the undoubted influence of this religion in the founding of Buddhism, Christianity and Islam. We talked about this point for some time before giving a further chance to main speaker to conclude his speech. "However," he continued, "we admit that he was a great thinker and tried to teach people to be better persons but that is all, nothing else. To be honest with you," he added rather stubbornly, "even if

41

we reluctantly concede that, the intention of all founders of religions was constructive, and they categorically meant to introduce systems of education for the good of humanity, we would still fail to find any association between such a generous hypothesis and the existence of your God, full stop."

*

"As for Buddhism" one of the intellectuals took over in a different meeting with obvious sign of respect and care in handling this round, "it begins with a man called 'Gautama' who was born in 563 BC to an affluent family and lived until 483 BC. When he was a young man, he left the riches and his wife behind and for years practiced all methods of recluses, experienced austerity and self-denial and suffered hardships; hoping that he would attain Enlightenment and Nirvana but, bitterly failed to achieve his objective. He then gave up the austerity and mortifications and adopted the middle way in his private life, that is to say neither living in poverty nor in luxury." Here again the debater noticed that he may fall in similar trap as his colleague if continued the style he had started with, and so continued with a clear intention of mocking the event that he was about to describe. "One night, while he was sitting under a big tree seriously contemplating the mysteries of the life and what he had gone through to accomplish his objective, suddenly, and out of blue, he attained the enlightenment and not just once but three times and apparently, each time as his highness claimed later on; he was raised to higher level and eventually he experienced the Nirvana. Following this, Gautama announced that he was the Buddha, the awakened one, and set to teach his method of attaining the enlightenment and reaching the Nirvana, to others." We continued to talk and emphasized that Buddha opposed the self-mortification as a way for self-development and attaining Nirvana. Therefore, to begin with there was no place for self-denial and any other kind of ascetic practices in Buddhism but, after a few centuries believers of this religion slowly succumbed to the similar practices or worse. "Although Buddhism as a religion," said the speaker, "or a way of life started from the Gautama's teachings but, according to scriptures he was not the first Buddha. Some refer to him as the number 8 and others as Buddha number 28. Certain branches of Buddhism regard Brahman as the first Buddha." He smiled and said, "Should we give it up, sir?" I encouraged him to continue as I had become interested to find out, why he could not hide his obvious respect for this religion in spite of trying to ridicule the whole idea. "Here again," he went on to say; "the main aim is realizing the enlightenment and Nirvana. No one is bothered about God. In fact the Buddhism is considered as non-theistic religion anyway." When he mentioned the point of atheism within this religion (as far as he could perceive) I realised why the intellectuals had shown so much respect to Buddhism. This was confirmed with further discussion about Buddhism. "Having said so" he continued, "there are numerous divisions, branches and schools in this religion too.   Some of the major schools consider Buddha as god of all gods or indeed the God himself in human form. They seriously believe in Buddha's eternity and his indestructibility and very much hope that he would come again in another human body (as incarnated God) when the world needs him."   Here our funny friend said, "I'm surprised by the founders of Christianity.   They could easily pretend that not only was Jesus the promised Messiah of the Jews but also, he was the promised Buddha of the Buddhists."   The speaker ignored him again as it had become an accepted pattern to be interrupted by the joker. "Now the followers worship Buddha's statutes and paintings, at home or in temples and shrines. They offer gifts and food and burn incense for him which is back to idolatry in my view.   You can't win my dear friend, people love worshiping and one way or other, they will find an idol to worship; whatever you do.   This is an important point that we will come back to when we talk about your God. However, their methods of attaining the enlightenment is different but today most monks continue to beg for their one daily meal and alms. I suppose it is part of their effort for humility and self-development," smiled the infidel. "In that case our beggars in the town stand much better chance for enlightenment," observed the funny intellectual, "after years of their hard work begging." But the rest of listeners were too serious about their debates to take any notice of him and so speaker went on talking. "It is interesting to note the obvious signs of influence that old religions, especially Zoroastrianism had on Buddhism. Examples are abstaining from the disagreeable actions of body and mind, practicing the right speech, right action and right thoughts that have become part of their teaching for self-development. Having said that in spite of the fact that many ideas and practices have been copied from Zoroastrianism and Brahmanism, the Buddhism is a religion in its own right." As if he had discovered something he looked quite pleased with himself. I wondered whether he knew how many Buddhist are in the world when he reluctantly said, a religion in his own right. "Well," said he rather triumphantly, "this one was not a difficult case at all, basically because it is a non-theistic religion anyway. But once again it just illustrates that religions are the ideologies of philosophers, sociologists and politicians that were put forward in order to govern upon the people and lead them based on their ideas regarding the social and personal lives and have nothing to do with God. This is indeed an excellent example for you my friend," said the speaker, looking at me with sympathy "here we are taking about the fourth or fifth biggest religion in the world in which not only the founder does not claim to have been sent by God, he does not believe in him either." "If founders of all religions were as honest as Buddha," said the observant joker, "we would not have so much trouble in the world today." And that was the end of our discussion about Buddhism, rather prematurely I thought. There was lots of hot news about the underground activities against the Shah's regime and about arrests. There were rumours of more executions inside the prisons too and so not all the talks were about the religious matters. However, from time to time, we would come back to that issue too. One night having exchanged the information about political activities one of our friends remembered their duty to save me. "By the way," he began to enlighten me, "there have been too many cults in history and surely more will come later. Someone claims to have been sent by God as a prophet or is the incarnated God. Then several thousand or even millions of people believe in him or her and are prepared to give and do whatever the so called prophet or incarnated God wants." The new speaker knew that, I didn't see myself in a state of mind and intellect to believe in such prophets or gods therefore we did not spend time in these examples either. We did observe of course, that they are false prophets and professional charlatans, who take advantage of the naivety and simplicity of innocent people to establish false religions only for their own interests. I was aware that throughout history many individuals have successfully made such claims and

48

attracted fanatic followers. I had heard about their exceptional talent to influence the minds of the people. I was also aware of a sad example in which the leader of cult had ordered mass suicide to his followers and, all those brain washed and devoted devotees of this leader had happily murdered their own children and killed themselves in hundreds. For those cults, prophets or gods the intellectuals did not need to exert themselves to prove their absurdity to me but probably they thought that, it was necessary to mention in order to pave their way for main religions and God himself. At this stage most members of our society were pleased to have such an easy going hesitant monotheist so; they looked at each other triumphantly and, drank more wine to wish me health and prosperity. They were keen to close the subject in hand as soon as possible and get on with our major undertaking, which was establishing democracy in the country. I honestly laugh when I remember those days. What a huge agenda we had; to destroy the religions, reject the God, get rid of the king of kings (as Shah used to be addressed) and establish democracy in the country and all of these from the comfortable room of Café Naderi over a few cups of coffee or few glasses of wine. However, in general discussions we mentioned that unfortunately throughout the history of man, those in power and rulers; have used religions and God, to rob the people with taxes, donations and sacrifices. Indeed, by taking advantage of their innocent faiths they have exploited them. Sadly throughout the history, in the name of God tyrants have justified their atrocities and vices. They are doing precisely the same at present time and will continue to do so in future. Many nights we had discussions along the same lines and reached to similar conclusions and then, they began destroying the big ones, having swallowed alcohol more than the previous nights to sharpen their minds.

"There are three main universal religions left to destroy," began one of my saviours, "and now, we will describe them to illustrate to you; how they were invented and why they would not help you to accept God on their grounds. The oldest one is Judaism." But having seen a question mark on my face; he tried to explain, "Okay, it isn't universal religion so to speak. But, nevertheless it is one of the oldest and the most troublesome one in history." "Indeed it is," said the joker with obvious signs of dislike on his face, "and will continue to cause even more troubles as it gets older." Unlike the previous times, the speaker agreed with our comedian and then added on, "To begin with the fact is that there is not a single mention of a person called Abraham, in any historical documents, apart from biblical ones of no historical value and the Quran. As for the Moses, it is true that his name has been mentioned in a few history books but it appears that they are referring to an Egyptian priest, who became the leader for a group of people in Egypt who for some reason were discontented there. The biblical related books have claimed that, Abraham (the first prophet) lived from 19 to 18 century

BC apparently for 175 years, if you can believe it. And Moses lived during 13 and 12 century BC. The compilation of The Old Testament was completed 800 to1000 years after the claimed time of Moses, and is therefore not reliable in its accuracy. After such a long delay and without any valid record how could scribes know of the events at the time of Moses or the nature of his teachings and guidance? More likely the stories of ancient scriptures and the laws within them were cleverly invented by some rabbis and scribes which became a bestseller due to their exciting stories of wars, violence, evil plots and crimes." "Indeed," continued the self-reliant historian, "believing that God sent Abraham, Isaac, Jacob, Moses and many other Jewish prophets, to establish a religion and protect it; is absurd. Although one has to acknowledge that clever rabbis have managed to protect a form of it anyway. What may have happened is that, Moses led mass of the discontented and uncivilized people out of the main land of Egypt and marched towards Palestine, which belonged to the

Egyptians but it was too far away to be controlled by the central government." "Well," he went on after another interruption by our joker, "during their long voyage, Moses had to establish some kind of organisation, laws, rules and regulations in order to control the ungovernable people." The infidel was narrating the story so confidently that one wondered whether he himself was present there at the time of that march witnessing the events. "To do this Moses copied the new policy of worshiping only one major god (out of many gods and goddesses available). So he invented his own major god with a different name of course and terrorised his people with the wrath of that god, and his revenge or punishment, if they dared to worship any other god. In fact Moses was not a monotheist as one understands today and his main purpose of such an idea was to present a personal god and identity to his people. He had also realized that threatening with the wrath of his god is the best and perhaps the only way that he could keep his people in order. And this policy has continued by other prophets and religious leaders throughout the history." This point was debated in length and turned to a political argument but, the speaker managed to lead the conversation to where his narration had been disrupted. "The people were persuaded and indeed forced to believe that all the laws which Moses set and all the orders and guidance that he brought to them actually came from God himself. From then onwards any disobedience of the laws or believing in any other god received the most severe punishment and most ruthless revenge, all of which apparently came directly from the Moses' newly manufactured god or carried out to his orders. Yes, Moses was a leader and legislator but not a prophet," concluded the speaker, "and the rest of the story you've read in books yourself and know that, his laws gradually became a religion for the Israelites."

I had read different versions of that story and, was aware of what the speaker was talking about but I found his views quite simplistic and clearly heavily influenced by his profound contempt of this religion. I said so but remained interested and patient to hear more about the rest of the story to find out how are we going to reject God by dismissing this religion, even if we could. The intellectual, who had taken the task of destroying Judaism, went on to connect his arguments with the question of God. "Let us assume that Abraham, Moses and rest of the gang established this religion by the order of God. It is evident from their scriptures that Judaism and its doctrine were extended to one nation only, not to all humans and God belongs to the Israelites alone. He is the same God, as the scriptures claim, who promised them a land, which created such a complicated problem that even today it remains unresolved and it is one of the main obstacles to the peace on earth." "It is all Cyrus' fault," said the comical man half-jokingly, "because, he is the very person who freed the Jewish captives in Babylon and, sent them back into Palestine, to rebuild their holy city and write their scriptures. Had he been a bit economic in generosity we would not have inherited such a devastating conflict in Middle East and its never ending consequences." He was referring to the historical fact of freeing the Israelites from the Babylon captivity by Persian king Cyrus the great. "But seriously speaking," said the main destroyer, "does such a religion prove the existence of your one and only God, who created the entire universe and belongs to all human beings? Don't you see resemblance between this God and gods of the Idolaters? Is it not similar to theistic beliefs of the ancient nations and primitive tribes of past? They too had their own manufactured gods and goddesses belonging just to one tribe or a nation. You see my friend, it does not prove your view because there is no universal God and everyone wants to invent and possess his or her own personal, tribal or national god." I was already put off by what I had read in old scriptures, and, I could see some of the points he was making but, I was not prepared and did not want to use inaccuracy and absurdity of the matters written in the sacred books and the absurdity of some of religious beliefs to reject God.

*

"As for the Christianity," one of the intellectual began in a different meeting, "first of all some researchers have serious doubt that, a person called Jesus has ever existed at all but I want to believe that he existed and base our discussion on the interesting story that has been told. However, before I begin scrutinising the story I must mention that, there is a striking similarity between 'ancient human gods' and 'Jesus' but I cut it short here and may return to that point in future meetings." He paused for a minute and then continued, "Let us face it. Although the architects of Christianity have succeeded in either amending or eliminating some of absurdities of the earlier religion and mistakes of its creators for example transforming God to tangible, kind and lovable character but at the same time, they have produced greater problems for any independent and just thinker to accept. "Anyway," continued the storyteller having swallowed a glass of wine ready to describe a lengthy story, "it all started from Mary becoming pregnant." He then talked in details (quite un-necessary I thought), about the alleged sexual relationship of a young man named Joseph ben-Pandora who was apparently a soldier in their neighbourhood with Mary, while the other Joseph, her husband, was away. "To do justice," said the intellectual, "it is most likely the young soldier deceived Mary and it is even possible that, he actually pretended to be an angel carrying mission from God hence; foundation of the subsequent claim about the virginity of Mary and the rest of the story. This clever claim worked very well indeed, because already there was a prophecy in the ancient Jewish traditions that one day a Messiah (or a saviour) born from a virgin mother, will come to save the Israelites."

My saviours, were doing their very best, to fulfil the promise of rescuing me from the doubts and uncertainties with no effect until then. "Yes," said the infidel, "for many years Jews were expecting a Messiah to emerge, establish a Mighty Empire, help them to rise against the Romans and return their stolen liberty and independence. For too long the Israelites were dreaming of conquering the other nations and establishing a Jewish kingdom, above all the empires on earth. Yes they were dreaming of ruling the whole world and still do." At this point another intellectual offered additional information. "It is interesting to note that," he said, "the belief in virgin birth was already amongst the other religions and nations, for example Mithraism. This is a religion that originated from Persia; probably by product of Zoroastrianism and became formal religion of Roman Empire for three hundred years. In this religion" he went on, "it was claimed that Mithra (sun god) was also born from virgin mother on a rock." "That is right," said the previous speaker eagerly, "but before I forget, I must add that, being born from a virgin mother is not the only likeness between Christianity and Mithraism. Baptism in holy water was also practiced in Mithraism long before John started it which later on was adapted by Christians. It is obvious that John learned this practice from either Mithraism or perhaps other religions and brought it to the land of Israelites. However, whatever is the story the fact is that Mary's pregnancy was before the beginning of a marital relationship with her husband. When her husband (Joseph) returned home and discovered that his wife was pregnant he became very upset and angry. First he decided to divorce her but he knew well that, the penalty for adultery was very heavy. He really loved Mary and could not see her killed in this way so he decided to flee that area and live somewhere else."

I did not think that the story of this infidel was a proven historical fact although versions of such an interpretation are recorded in some books. He continued with his line of the story disregarding my objection. "However, she gave birth to Jesus and went on to have more children from her husband. And so, there is no way that Mary could have been or remained virgin whether in her first pregnancy or subsequent ones unlike what Christians claim." The infidel laughed heartily and appeared proud of his new discovery and continued with the narration, as assured as before. "His Jewish parents in poverty raised Jesus as a Jew and although an illiterate peasant, he turned out to be a smart and conscientious young man. He soon noticed immense corruption amongst the Jewish priests and kings and began his brave campaign and struggle, against the establishment at the time. He preached diligently and made people aware of ruler's oppressions and the fact that, rabbis had added new laws to religion only to protect their own gains and interests." As he continued to talk; we learnt that rabbis had included excessive rituals, ceremonies and false traditions; essentially to support and augment their own glories and defend their positions. Indeed Jesus believed that, Jewish priests were too anxious about small details of rituals and had forgotten their far more important duties, regarding morality

61

and the spiritual aspects of the teachings. "In the opinion of Jesus," said the speaker, "those rabbis' religious understanding extended no further than rites and ceremonies."

When we were talking about the Christianity the interesting point that I noticed was the way they referred to Jesus. Most of the intellectuals referred to him with the highest respect and love and were considering him a revolutionary, a hero. As a matter of fact one of them with genuine grief said, "Corrupted Jewish rabbis plotted against Jesus Christ many times and finally, managed to hand him over to Romans to be crucified. Jesus died for the principles that he believed in. Like our friends who die under the tortures (in prisons) or are executed for defending the weak and oppressed people." The speaker agreed with him and added, "Yes, Jesus was a hero but not the son of God. He was a man and many times he had mentioned this but politics made him a God." The joker interrupted again by saying, "His disciples called him son of

God so many times that, towards the end of his brief life even poor Jesus believed it." "Years later," continued the speaker, "some of his disciples and politicians used the good name of this dearly loved man and the story of his life and painful crucifixion, together with his widely distorted and extensively edited teachings; to establish a religion that to begin with was merely a Jewish cult, no more. One of the disciples (Peter I think) was the person who kept calling Jesus son of God, more than anybody else even though; Jesus had repeatedly declared otherwise. And it is this Peter, assisted by Paul, who eventually achieved his big ambition of establishing a mighty empire by founding a new religion, building the churches and introducing sacramental practices, during the first century AD even though Jesus himself was against establishing an earthly empire." At this point the speaker delivered a long description of curious visions and practices of uncivilised and primitive people which had begun thousands of years before Jesus Christ was born. He described how they slew their own invented human gods, drank their blood, ate their flesh, spread gods' blood or, buried parts of their body in the cultivated lands, like a fertiliser as well as a blessing for the copious crop of corn etc. These primitive people would see the growth of corn as resurrection of their slain god.   They believed that by eating the body of God and drinking his blood you absorb his divinity, he and you become one person and so he is always in you and inspires you. In other words they believed such a horrible practice was for their own salvation. The intellectual also explained the annual ritual of killing of a man as temporary representative of their slain god, to sacrifice for him in order to keep god's spirit around for the protection.   In such annual ceremonies; they drank poor victim's blood too and ate his flesh or buried pieces of his body exactly repeating what they had done when they slew their god in the first place.   Later on of course as the people became relatively civilised they slew animal substitute to spare the human.   These practices evolved further and they began eating the bread (resembling their god's body) and drinking wine (as his blood) for the same blessings and protection that they had assumed received it, when they slew their main god or substitutes. The intellectual wanted to draw my attention to remarkable similarities between what primitive people did, in ancient time and the story of Jesus' Crucifixion as well as sacramental practices at present time. "However," added supposedly well informed infidel, "it seems that being just son of God was not enough for their purpose and plans so, once Christianity spread abroad and got to as far as Egypt the founders of this new religion, having heard about Trinity of Osiris, Isis and Horus; decided to give a Trinitarian shape to their new religion too. They presented the Father (God) the Son (Jesus) and Holy Spirit as one entity and from that period, effectively Jesus was worshiped as God." Here, one of the intellectuals added that, "The question of Trinity had already been established in other religions too and was not confined to Egyptians nor it was the discovery of inventors of Christianity, if they so claim. For example Brahman the highest god of

Brahmanism is perceived as Trinity consisting of Brahma, Vishnu and Shiva. It is also true to say that in Buddhism; Supreme Spirit, Holy Spirit and Incarnated Spirit are seen in Buddha as Buddhist Trinity."

"My dear friend," said the concerned intellectual, "I'm afraid you will not find your one only universal God here either; because even in such an undisputed universal religion of our time, initially accepted monotheism was totally abandoned and practically Christians adopted polytheism, not only by copying the Trinity of Egyptians but also, by worshiping Mary as goddess and later on, numerous manufactured live or dead saints. What else can I tell you?" asked the infidel, "Several ideas and rituals from Egyptian's religions were borrowed and with certain alterations were added to their newly created religion. Even the painters copied their subjects of paintings from Egyptian artists and put (the child Jesus) on Mary's arm or lap exactly like Horus (the child god) that, was habitually painted while sitting on the lap of Iris (the goddess). Anyway," said the speaker after a long pause, "The Roman Empire had Mithraism as their main religion for hundreds of years and lots of other religions amongst different nations living in the same empire, initially opposed the Christianity and prosecuted or even murdered many activists or simple faithful Christians. But later on, they happily helped the plan to succeed as they recognised that this ingenious idea of having a brand new and potentially universal religion introduced by the tangible God himself is extremely an attractive one. Indeed, Romans appreciated that, such a move not only would help them to unite the various nations living in the country under newly invented religion, but also, it would lead to their domination of the whole world when the centre of the new religion is Rome. And the move once again worked very well." The speaker talked about political conditions of the era and readiness of the people, to accept a new religion particularly that they could see similarities with their own religions (the religions that were already fading away). He then went on to say, "The inventers of this new religion had most cleverly included many ideas and practices from not only Mithraism or religion of Egyptians but also, from Hinduism, Zoroastrianism and Buddhism in order to present this brand new religion acceptable for all the nations and the product was a huge triumph.   However Jews did not accept Jesus Christ as the expected Messiah after all simply because; he did not look like the prince they were looking for and he did not promise them to establish an earthly empire which they were hoping for. So, they did not take their chance but clever Romans did." At this stage, the narrator having talked in detail about the rise of Christianity and likeness with other faiths of the time (because of inclusion of materials in it) looked very tired and therefore another infidel took over the subject.

"For years Mithraism and Christianity lived side by side in Roman Empire only because people were not happy to give up worshiping of Mithra (the sun god). To solve this problem Roman Politicians and Christian Religious leaders thought of a clever trick. They chose Mithra's birthday 25 December for the birthday of Jesus and assigned Sundays for praying of Christians in churches as in Mithraism it was called Lord's day, (because of the association of Mithra with sun) and it was already the day of worship for most Romans. Soon after such a clever move, Christianity became the official religion of the super power of those days." The former non-believer having restored his strength with a glass of wine returned to his duty and changed the subject, trying to draw his talks to a conclusion. "As for the writing of New Testament, although the delay was not as lengthy as the Old one but it took at least a hundred years or more, before the Gospels were written by different persons on different dates and it took several hundred more years before those materials were compiled in a book. It is important to note that, the authors of New Testament accepted the Old Testament and also borrowed a few ideas from Brahmins' book of Bhagava-Gita that was written on first or second century before Jesus was born. The Gospel writers have grossly contradicted each other and there have been many genuine mistakes in translations from Greek or Hebrew to other languages and there have been many misinterpretations which make most part of the story unauthentic and unreliable. The reality is that," he finally concluded, "Christianity is a blend of several ideas from different religions with all the subsequent additions or alterations in it. Christianity, like any other main religion has many divisions and branches and while some of the divisions are natural consequences of alterations in teachings of Jesus most of them are for political purposes."

It was fascinating to find, how differently one could look at the issues and how everyone thinks he is right and others wrong. But what mattered to me was the question of God and so I showed my readiness to hear more and patiently waited to be enlightened further and released from doubt as they had promised. "My friend," said the intellectual confidently, "I don't wish to talk about the so-called miracles of Jesus Christ as I know well that, today no rational mind will accept such claims. But I do say this," he hesitated for a minute and then continued, "neither the claim of Jesus being Son of God, nor the beautiful story that, they have manufactured, nor the religion that long after the crucifixion of Jesus has been established; prove the existence of God." And by such a final statement they ended the discussion about Christianity.

*

When we got to Islam it was clear that they were very cautious. This was because of undeclared alliance with the Islamists' movement against the Shah. It was not long ago, when the first major rebellion of Khomeini's followers had been inhumanly quashed by Shah's iron fist but, underground activities of the religious and nonreligious parties continued. Obviously, a united front of left and right was beginning to emerge as all the concerned parties had recognized that struggling against such a dictatorship, needed more than just one section of the freedom fighters. So, it was tactically essential for the intellectuals of our society to be cautious. However, in spite of this consideration, in one of the meetings a new speaker began talking about the fact that, like Jesus, "Mohammad" was also illiterate and therefore, most likely a Persian called Salman Farsi, who was a smart and educated man and always accompanied the Prophet; was the person behind the commended beauty of language used in Quran, which is indeed more like poetry. We noted that although "The Quran" is the only holy book which was written whilst the Prophet himself was still alive and was compiled in a book, almost immediately after his death, it is far from being intact. Some parts of it, which were not in the best interest of powerful and rich rulers, might have been omitted and some might have been altered. We ridiculed the contents of the books named "solution to the problems" which are generally written by highly ranked religious leaders. We laughed at the rules and regulation of entering into the toilet, whether you put your left foot first or the right. We were amazed to read that whether you could eat the meat of your own cow if you had sex with it or should you sell this victim of the sexual abuse to one of your neighbours? There was even a hot debate about the pronunciation of certain words of the prayer; should they come from the depth of your throat or front of your mouth. We laughed for a long time when one of the gang quoted a promise in one of these books that when you are in Heaven you will have beautiful women with breasts as big as a mountain. We could not understand mentality of the priest and his definition of the beauty of women. These are only examples of the absurd matters in books written by priests (mullahs). One of the intellectuals referred to various narratives or traditions that have been attributed to Prophet Mohammad which majority are surely false. "These are called Hadith," he explained, "and most likely have been manufactured to protect the interests of religious leaders or wealthy people and rulers. Indeed, they have been heavily used for this purpose since Prophet died. Researchers have shown that out of the three hundred thousand of Hadiths, only seven thousand might be correct". "The Prophet knew that such problem would arise after his death," said a new member of our society who was a religious young man, "so, he warned Moslems before his death". He was not happy about the way Islam was discussed amongst us, even though I thought it was quite restrained, but had not objected openly. I suppose he too, had realised that upholding the united front alive and continuation of the coalition of right and left, in such a crucial time of the struggle, is by far more important than arguing about the tone of discussion. However, this young man was referring to the fact that Mohammad had said to the Moslems, "After my death, the sayings attributed to me will multiply fast, just as large number of them is attributed to other prophets before me. So, when you hear a saying presented to you as one of mine you must compare it with Quran and only if it was in agreement with the content of Quran then it is from me, otherwise not." "Like Judaism and Christianity," continued the intellectual even though, he was conscious of sensitivity of issue after being interrupted, "there are many added rituals or ceremonies and superstitious beliefs in Islam too that has distracted the worshipers from spiritual and moral teachings of Quran. And it is true to say that there are many divisions and subdivisions in Islam too like any other religions." The infidels reminded us that Quran like Old Testament has frightened the people from wrath of God and we also concluded that here again those in power have used this religion to protect their own benefits and for political purposes. Finally they concluded that although Islam is the only universal religion that strictly believes in only one God but its holy book Quran has repeated most of the ingredients of the Old and New Testaments and does not add anything more to admit God's existence. Having said that we recognized that there are some realistic materials in The Quran such as referring to Jesus with the highest regards but presenting him as merely a blessed human who was the prophet of God. "Here again," declared the speaker as last observation, "We have the same problem as in Christianity which is worshiping of the saints alongside the God."

For many days and nights we talked about religions, rituals and ceremonies. We felt miserable to acknowledge that religious leaders have immense power in societies and unfortunately have great ability in using people for their political purposes as well as their immediate interests and gains.

*

Having finished with almost all the religions and faiths, the intellectuals presented me with an overall conclusion. They said, "Religions are the opium of the nations," a phrase that was borrowed from the Marxists, "Religions are established to make ruling people easier. Religions are there to keep them satisfied and hopeful for better life in next world. It is there to keep them happy with prospect of entering into Heaven and enjoy absolute peace, abundant food, wine and of course, most beautiful women or handsome men if new dwellers of Heaven were women. Religions are there to make the acceptance of inequalities in society easier for the people. They are there to fool ordinary people that inequalities are not the fault of rulers or ruling system and, there are no discriminations or tyranny committed by the powerful, as it is purely the will of God; to whom he gives more and to whom less. Religions are there to make the people passive, submissive to rulers and obedient of the religious leaders. In fact to please the Roman authorities; the founders of Christianity added the obedience of the rulers to the teachings of Jesus that he had never said so." I had a lot of sympathy with some of the points they were making but I thought that, after many sessions of the debates and arguments my uncertainty about existence of God remained the same as before. The main reason for remaining in almost the same state as before was that, I could neither visualise nor understand, how on earth by proving falsehood of religions even if we could prove it, one could conclude that God does not exist. I also sympathised with their remarks implying that the doctrines of religions precisely like any other philosophical, moral, social or political ideologies could have been put forward by the ideologists for good or evil purpose in their mind or perhaps to shape their societies according to their belief. If that was the case then one could accept that; God did not send the prophets and indeed religions have got nothing to do with him. But again, I could not see how such an argument could lead to the denial of God. We cannot reject God, just because he had no role in the establishment of religions. We cannot reject God only because we believe that our rational analysis proves that he did not send any prophets or messengers. I simply could not appreciate the links between the proof of absurdity of religions or, falsehood of the prophets with nonexistence of God and I argued so.   In spite of it, the infidels were not too disappointed with the results of debates because, they thought that, they had achieved enough for their mission and have more convincing arguments against the case of God, for our next round of which we were going to commence.

At this stage of the journey although most of my time was occupied by the extensive courses of basic sciences, (exclusive for first three years of Medical School) but I was anxious to continue with the meetings hoping that one way or other, I would arrive to firmer convictions and free myself from the agony of doubts and uncertainties.   I was desperately looking forward for peace of mind if at all doubts could be removed, so that I could concentrate on my education alongside the political activities in which I had become deeply involved.   The intellectuals were anxious to convince me as well as some of the newly recruited young religious members, so that, they too could concentrate on the main target that had brought us together in the first place, which was of course bringing freedom and democracy to our country and people. However, the reality is that nothing dramatic had changed in my condition because, doubts and uncertainties had remained as tormenting as before, if not more so and my thirst to read the books and seek the Truth hidden somewhere inside them had not subsided. I must confess of course, that (as the intellectuals had also noticed and considered it as a success for first round) my faith in religions had weakened a great deal but as mentioned earlier I would not deny God merely because of what I thought of them. This was the situation after the first round of meetings and debates, which took some time to conclude. Regarding the next round of meetings that the intellectuals had promised to offer more convincing reasons I have to admit that, they were right as will be illustrated in the next chapter, but I must say, they were also lucky because of emergence of other factors in my life which had profound effect on my beliefs, overall.

Chapter 4

There is no God

Regular meetings with intellectuals of café Naderi continued as before but I remained the same old hesitant monotheist.   Having said that the things were gradually changing for me and many other factors, stronger than the arguments and influence of intellectuals were emerging in my life to put an end to uncertainties.   During the political activities, I developed an interest in Socialism that did not make believing in God any easier.   I became very hostile towards anything and anyone who was the perpetrator of crime, injustice and oppressions within the society or, had the means and power to prevent them but did not do so and this included Omnipotent God himself.   I was in such a state of mind and turmoil that far more serious debates about the God began in our meetings.   One of the intellectuals with a determined attitude opened the new round of debate by declaring, "The first human beings lived in great danger, among the wild and strong animals, in both daylight and darkness, while desperately struggling to cope with hunger, thirst and extremes of the climate.   And all these with no protection, help or support and indeed with no shelter except for the dark and damp caves that were themselves frightening places to live.   They were living in constant fear of natural disasters and were extremely frightened of being alone.   Even today, at least some of the subconscious fears that we have, originate from the ancient times; because we have inherited through our genes, the lonely fears of our ancestors' mind. Surely, primitive man ought to have been trying to find a remedy for their problem?   Well," continued the atheist, "they found it. Humans created god in their mind in order to take refuge, to have company and to whom appeal for help and support when it was needed.   Man needed a supernatural power for protection and help so, he created it.   And, when humans learned to use materials of nature and invented some instruments to work with; they began to give images of their gods and goddesses, by making them from clay, wood or stone. They placed their gods (idols) nearby, close to their dwellings in order to talk with, to ask for the support and protection when needed, or just worship them". Here he gave a long lecture followed by a heated argument that, like the other topics in the book I would not claim to be the whole debates. Obviously after so many years that passed I don't remember all that was said and have lost some of my notes but I do remember the followings.

*

"Some people began to worship the sacred animals or objects in nature. Gradually when they learned to live together, they made gods and goddesses collectively. Then dwelling places were made for gods. Each group of the people had either their own gods at home or worshiped the tribal or

85

national gods. Some had different gods and goddesses for various powers or things in the nature for example; a god or goddess of beauty, fertility, agriculture, food, fire, rain, light, peace and war. Thereafter, people began worshiping their dead parents, chieftains or kings as human gods." The atheist intellectual talked in details about the manufacturing of gods or goddesses by different groups or nations. He described how and why the idea of god and worship gradually evolved and man began worshiping not just the corpses of dead relatives, chieftains or kings but also their ghosts that, later on changed to worshiping stones laid on their graves or trees grown beside them. Having exhausted all the facts and myths about the most mysterious and vicious rituals and brutalities in relation to sacrificing of fellow humans for their gods he continued to describe how worshiping itself, evolved in due course.

"Yes my friend, in order to please their gods and goddesses; worshipers began donating food and gifts, offering human or animal sacrifices and paid regular homage to them. Soon, they began building tombs, temples, pantheons and shrines for their gods and goddesses and worshiping became even more ceremonial and ritual. Therefore," summed up the atheist, "fear and loneliness were the main factors that led to the invention of god by man. But having said that, we shouldn't forget the role of another crucial factor in emergence of the idea of god in their mind, and that is the natural affinity of man to rites and worship. I don't need to prove this point to you. Look around, if we didn't find a god to worship we will certainly find someone or something to adore. We make idols of actors or actresses, pop stars, sport persons or simply a beautiful woman and then dedicate ourselves to adore them. It seems that we are unable to enjoy life fully, without worshipping someone or something and clearly we love rites." My atheist friend could not stop talking, he was enjoying the opportunity. "However," said he, "gradually religions were also established (as we discussed earlier) and for each religion one or more gods were assigned. People wanted god and the makers of the religions gave it to them in variety of shapes and images. They either chose one god or more from the already invented and worshipped ones, if it was suitable for their plans, or, they made new ones in various shapes and forms of sacred stones or trees, sacred animals or sun, fire so on and so forth. Idolatry and polytheism lasted for a long time but it could not go on forever as, knowledge and rationalisation of humans had progressed and so believing in only one God seemed more logical. In this period to begin with, people worshipped one god out of the various already manufactured and accessible gods but later, worshiping of supreme and invisible God was encouraged. " The atheist continued to talk and harshly ridicule the concept of invisibility but, at the same time he had to acknowledge a major advance in the idea of theism. "Soon this type of theism found its popularity amongst the religious people and to be fair it made sense as well comparing with the irrationality of idolatry or polytheism and associated unbelievable rituals. But usually," said the atheist intellectual anxious to add another supposedly proven fact to support his debate, "most of people find it difficult to comprehend, accept or believe in something; without seeing, touching, hearing, tasting and smelling it, which is the main reason why humans invented the idols in the first place and, why idolatry was so easily accepted and survived for such a long period of time. Indeed a tangible god is so crucial for people that even today modern versions of idolatry that satisfies the above mentioned senses, has not completely disappeared and perhaps never will be. However," said the intellectual, "to solve such a practical problem, the ancient prophets claimed that they had seen God and talked to him. They explained to people that the God that they saw and talked to was a real one and different from previously idolized false ones." Here, once again the joker interrupted the course of narration to dismay of the speaker. "It sounds a better idea, in comparison I mean. But it is rather suspicious. Why should prophets be the only ones to see

God?" Speaker disregarding the joker continued his line, "So, in order to convince or deceive the innocent and simple people; they even defined the image of God and conveyed his directives to them and they also said ordinary people could not see him." He then added, "Here again such a method of convincing or fooling the people worked very well for some time but in the long term it too failed to satisfy them. And so the religious leaders and politicians, had to bring the God down on earth and show him to the people in man's own image; either as an incarnated form or otherwise." Our funny intellectual felt it necessary to interrupt the speaker again to remind me a point. "This is what we explained to you when religions were discussed. You will remember that after sending numerous prophets to teach or guide the people and having virtually failed to make them understand, what on earth they were talking about; your, omnipotent and omnipresent friend had no choice but to come down on earth in person." The main speaker who was not happy with his interruption paused for some time and then continued, "And this worked much better than the invisible God. A French philosopher once said, "If triangles had God, he would have had three sides. The Greek philosopher Xenophanes had made a similar comment more than 2000 years before the French philosopher. "If the bulls or lions made God they would make him in the form of bull or lion". And that was exactly what shrewd religious leaders and politicians thought of and presented an accessible God; (in man's own image) to the people and they rejoiced and loved him." At this point our joker said something so seriously which astonished us. "Problem had been solved for a good few centuries until Islam came in and summoned the people to worship only one invisible God, a God who created the whole universe and sent all of prophets including my dear hero Jesus to guide the people, Mohammad being last one of the prophets. This declaration of course threatened and virtually spoiled all the efforts and achievements of earlier religious leaders and politicians who had just managed to present a tangible and lovable God to the people with excellent result." The atheist speaker laughed and went on with his own speech. "My dear friend the truth is that there is no God, we created him. We invented him because we are weak creatures and need supernatural powers to help us. We invented him because we are afraid of being alone. We did it because our limited knowledge could not explain everything in nature, nor would answer the questions we were faced with and therefore we thought that it would be much easier to attribute all the questions or mysteries to God or some sort of supernatural powers. In other words, it was at least partly to cover up our ignorance." He also referred to Voltaire who had acknowledged the natural need of man to have a God by saying that, "if God did not exist, we would have invented him." and then in a philosophical gesture replied him as if, Voltaire was present in the meeting; "We have invented him my dear Voltaire, we have." And then he continued with the story of man creating God rather than God creating man.   "Anyway, once God was invented in the human's mind and various gods and goddesses were manufactured, those in power did not allow such a bright idea to fade away because, they too needed God but of course for totally different reasons.   They needed God to frighten people, to rule them, to exploit them and to keep them hopeful of receiving rewards in Heaven for their prayers, worship and obedience during their earthly lives."   The speaker made another pause to measure the effect of his explanations so far, and then continued with his task, "As the knowledge of man increased so did his expectations.   He wanted scientific answers for all his questions.   His main questions were how did the universe and life begin?   In the past such questions could not be answered so, to hide our failure of giving a logical answer, we said God created. But today, not only we can answer them; we can also explain everything else. We no longer need God or any supernatural power, do we?"   At this point our infidel lecturer rather flatteringly said, "My friend, you are a scientist yourself and soon you will be a qualified doctor. Can you honestly believe in something that existed long before universe came to existence? Could you really believe in something that was not created it-self? Or believe in something that cannot be seen and you call it God? By the way what was he doing before his creation? Was he bored and therefore created the universe as a toy to play with? Would you honestly believe in something that could neither be proved by logic nor by any scientific evidence? Besides, do you really need God?" The speaker having heard no reply from me answered himself. "Now that we have civilisation, laws and orders in the human societies we neither need to frighten people from the anger of God to make them righteous individuals and obedient of laws. Nor do we need to hide behind the supernatural powers when it comes to explanation of birth of the universe or the beginning of life."

*

In one of the meetings I told them of a dream that I had. I dreamed that I was flying and going up and up into the sky. There was nothing around me for a long period of time until I saw enormous circular steps which were extending to as far as eyes could see. It seemed that it was made from bluish marble and was covered by the thin fog.   There it was; the infinite sky, circular marble steps with thin fog on them, as simple as that.   And yet, it was the most beautiful scene I had ever seen in my life; indeed ineffable.   I stopped flying and began walking up the stairs while I had a feeling that, it must be God's palace.   As I was climbing up the stairs saturated with indescribable mixture of peace and happiness, as well as indescribable fear, I could see no one around me and, nothing but the never-ending steps.   Truly, I was horrified that I had flown that far from the earth but somehow I liked that strange fear. I did not want to return and indeed, I could not have done so even if I wanted to, as I had no idea how and where to return.   I was overwhelmed by an intense joy, fear and confusion. Then I saw an extremely handsome old man coming down the steps. Although he was just like any other human but at the same time, looked like pure light. For a few seconds, I thought he was God then I remembered that God is invisible. The old man appeared very kind and friendly person and therefore, I went to him and anxiously asked, "Where is God?" He seemed delighted to have seen an ordinary human being up there so he smiled and replied, "God is no longer here. Millions years ago he went to another universe." "What?" I cried shattered with the news, "Has he left us on our own here?" The old man looked at me with utmost affection and drew my attention to a plain box that I had failed to notice until then and said; "No God has not left man alone. He sees and hears everything through this box, don't you ever worry. You and everyone else on Planet Earth are connected to him through this beautiful box. Be assured he is in full command." My atheist friends listened attentively and said; "Well, that was only a dream. You think too much about God." "But it is a good sign," declared the joker, "your dream means that even if God existed at some point of the history, he is no longer here. You are one step closer to atheism." They all laughed heartily. Of course it was a dream or even hallucination I admitted, but it worried me a lot; what if it is true and God is no longer with us? "You are afraid of being alone, aren't you?" asked one of the atheists pitifully and made me to think about it for a long time.

The political activities intensified very rapidly, serious events multiplied and so, the subject of our meetings could no longer be only God. We were bombarded by the sad news of arrests, tortures and murders. Armed struggles of Marxist organisations had increased as well as the struggle of Islamic movements and these; had provided an excuse to autocratic regime to quash uprisings and resistance even harder. During first few years of the Medical School, in which beside study of the course I was politically more active, I saw at close hand the ugliness of imprisonment, intimidation and physical or psychological torture. I witnessed harsh interrogations and savage torture and I saw executions too. I also became aware of horrifying atrocities happening to the families of political prisoners. I heard from reliable sources and witnesses that, some of political prisoners who had resisted all kinds of tortures, refused to cooperate with the secret police and refused to disclose names of the leaders and other activists; had faced with the most inhumane and ruthless behaviour of the regime. The torturers had raped mothers, sisters, wives and children of the prisoners in front of them while Omnipresent God was right there (I supposed) enjoying himself by watching those shameful acts and taking no action against the perpetrators. I was extremely angry with God and could not understand his inaction in those situations. Yes, I too was imprisoned and although it was only for a short period of time but it was enough to have a first-hand experience of unbelievable cruelties of the human to his fellow creatures. In that short confinement, from dark, cold, damp and lonely corner of the prison cell I shouted at the God; are you deaf and blind?" And that was not my only problem with God in those torturous dark days. I saw the poor families and the ultra-rich ones too. I saw the hungry children and those who were bursting from excess of food. I saw oppressed people and cruel oppressors and I asked, why on earth God does not prevent such cruelties, atrocities and injustices? If God exists and loves us I asked myself, why he has created so many bad people in the first place to commit these cruelties and oppressions. If everything we do is based on God's plan and merely with his will and approval we act, then why does he allow anyone to do wrong? If our destiny and what we do are written before hand and we could do nothing but with God's will, does it mean that no criminal or oppressor should ever be blamed or punished for their deeds, and all is God's own fault and responsibility? And why do the oppressors, whether ordinary ones or those in a ruling system, get away with all their crimes and vices seeming happier and stronger all the time. But the poor oppressed people become weaker and weaker and ever more miserable? Does God really exist and see everything yet does nothing about it, or is it true that there is no God and we have made him up ourselves? Perhaps my friends are right; we have created him not the other way around. I was extremely angry about the inequalities and social injustice. I was dismayed and indeed utterly disappointed that not only had God not prevented the atrocities of history but it seemed to me, that he was essentially siding with those worldwide oppressors and criminals or at least lets them get away with their crimes. This volatile state of mind and my emotional sensitivity coincided with the period that the theory of Big Bang had been widely accepted and had become every child or adult's subject of talk. At the same time, I had just finished a yearlong course of comparative anatomy, (it was within the curriculum of Medical Schools in those days) and for the third time I had read Darwin's theory of evolution.

Combination of these factors together with the influence of those atheist intellectuals and, my own readings but above all my anger at God's inaction; ended the uncertainties and I declared, "There is no God." In the last meeting that God was discussed we confidently concluded that, we do not need supernatural powers to answer our questions anymore and there is no place or need for God, as we can now explain everything logically and scientifically. Therefore, we arrogantly explained two main questions (birth of the universe and the beginning of life on earth), that a summary of it is more and less as below, of course, the way we understood in those days.

*

Billions years ago; when matter was condensed in one place, a gigantic explosion that we now call the Big Bang occurred, which led to formation of billions of stars and planets within the millions of galaxies. It happened that in one of these Galaxies our planet within our solar system; had exceptional physical and chemical conditions, to produce the first living thing in the form of a single cell. From then onwards as Darwin has explained, evolution took place during which after millions of years eventually man was evolved; as simple as that.   When we rehearsed this brief explanation of beginnings, the joker said, "This is a much better theory, isn't it? Compare it with religious account of making the man from clay and blowing soul in it. Honestly, which one sounds logical to you?"   "Therefore," continued the main debater proudly, "These theories of Big Bang and Evolution explain everything about the universe and life. It doesn't seem that there is a place for a creator. The fact is that there is no God and universe was not his creation in six days," he said rather sarcastically, "requiring him to rest on the seventh day."

And so we ended the discussions about the God.   I was officially accepted as an atheist in the society of infidels and immediately I felt its effect; the arrogance. Surely, they had freed me from distressing feelings of doubts and uncertainties but had filled me up with selfishness and arrogance; I was quite inflated. From that moment onwards I felt that I was well above religious people. I looked down on them and pitied them for their ignorance, inferiority and naivety. My father died and in my sorrow of such loss I also felt pity for him. I remembered that, many times I had heard him praying in the middle of night, intimately talking to God as if he was sitting beside him in room. In these occasions I even heard him crying. What a good man was my father I thought, but a very simple one too. Crying in the middle of night at such an age seemed strange to me. Why was he crying? Indeed what for? I kept asking myself. Was it the ecstasy attained from finding himself at the presence of God and seeing his light? But there is no God so, whom did he talk to? Probably it was just hallucination, I thought. When I think of those wasted years of my life I am pretty sure that the main factor and perchance the only factor that, led to the rejection of God was my emotional state as I was utterly distressed, furious, confused and agonizingly disappointed to see the apathy of our Omnipotent God.   I could not ignore his insensitivity or inaction in relation to injustices, atrocities and crimes throughout the world. Of course, it sounds very silly now but, it seems that in those days I was actually taking my revenge from an unjust God that in my view his function as God was totally unacceptable and indeed unforgivable.   My denial of God at that stage of the journey could not have been a true conviction.   I can honestly find no explanation for my conclusion in those dark days except for a childish way to take my revenge on him.   It sounds so stupid and embarrassing, I must confess.   I denied God because he ignored the tears on the faces of poor and hungry children. I denied God because he took no notice of the agony and misery of the victims of torture and rape, would not use his power to prevent corruption and crimes in human societies and all these failures demonstrated his utmost insensitivity and arrogance.   He ignored all the sufferings of mothers and wives of political prisoners and was not prepared to see or hear cries of those victims of oppression and atrocity who were desperately asking for help.   Having said so, I also remember quite clearly that even then; at the height of my fury, I was not entirely content with the theories regarding the birth of universe and origin of life on earth, as sufficient answers to our questions and acceptable explanation of mysteries. So, the main question remained unanswered; "How did all of these come into existence"?   Once again, something or perhaps someone deep inside me, was working hard to wake me up. But I deliberately ignored the call.   I was too frustrated and annoyed with God to listen to any call in his defence or, take notice of any advice.   I could no longer accept or respect a God who in my view had sided with powerful, oppressors and criminals.   The intellectuals of Café Naderi were quite happy with the outcome of their debates because, not only they had saved me from the degenerating forces of religions and theism (as they claimed) but also, they had managed to bring some of the new members, to their way of thinking. I must mention that, the new associated members were mainly from the religious sections of resistance and struggles for democracy, whereas the original intellectuals of society were mostly from the left of the political spectrum and obviously they were anxious to reinforce their front; in anticipation of dominance of the religious front in predicted revolution and thereafter an unavoidable power struggle.

Chapter 5

There ought to be a designer

For a relatively short period of time it seemed that I was quite happy with the absence of doubt and uncertainty in my mind and I was content with my conclusions regarding the religions, faith and the nonexistence of God. I was enjoying my approved status amongst the intellectuals and arrogantly assumed that religious beliefs are for uneducated and simple ordinary people not for elite and educated individuals like us. I harshly ridiculed and laughed at the naivety and ignorance of these religious people; whenever I met them in the churches, mosques, temples or the shrines.   I felt sorry for their simplicity when I found them, carrying out bizarre rituals and ceremonies innocently hoping to book a room in Heaven, or at least acquire God's help for their difficulties, problems and miseries.   I was no longer after the Truth and, was not actively searching for the answers to principal questions either that, used to keep my mind busy. I was more involved and concerned about the political issues and materialistic realities of the life. I didn't bother about the so called spiritual or metaphysical world. But a number of factors did not permit such a disgraceful mentality to last for too long; the factors that affected my mind one after the other and resulted in major changes. A change of heart and mind was triggered by my old practice of reading books thoroughly and, contemplating on the topics as I read them which also applied to the books of basic science. I have already mentioned that the first three years of the course in Medical School was mainly basic science which was taught in detail and at the highest possible levels for those days. I found the subjects exceedingly interesting, truly stimulating and challenging. So I bought and borrowed many more scientific books to study; more than were required for the exams at school of medicine

In the subject of Biochemistry I was really surprised to find out that, a tiny change to the molecule of a substance produces massive alterations in its chemical and physical property. How these delicately balanced chemical substances govern thousands of biochemical processes, within the body of the living creatures as a whole and humans specifically and how they are regulated, refined and maintained.

In the field of Immunology I was fascinated by the function of white cells and memory that exists in the immune system. If a pathogenic organism or a foreign agent for the first time enters the body; the immune system recognises that the invader is not self and is harmful. Then it immediately surrounds the invader to minimise the threat for the time being while preparing the body for a long-term defence; by producing a specific antibody against the invader that may take a couple of weeks or more to be ready. The most interesting and incredible point for me was that if years later the same pathogenic organism or, foreign agent once again entered the same body, not only that the immune system recognises the invader but also, remembers that, in the past it had produced specific chemical substance against its old enemy and then without any delay pours out the existing antibody to defend and retain health. Exactly like switching on a ready to use but abandoned production line in a factory. My question was; how does the immune system recognise that, any invader is not from himself and how it knows that the invader is dangerous in the first place and how this system remembers that not only it had met such a stranger in the past but also there is already a ready to use production line against enemy that only needs to be switched on? In those days, we did not know how precisely our own memory worked, let alone the memory of white cells or other components of immune system. Of course, today scientists have offered some explanations. They have done so by using a computer based model or information-processing model to unravel mysteries of human memory. There is a biochemical theory suggesting that, memory is stored by biochemical changes at the synapses of nervous system, and there is a neural circuit theory, implying that there may be a specific circuit in the brain for every memory or even specific dendritic growth and so on. But the fact is that we are still far from precise explanation and convincing answer to explicit question of how we remember? Equally, there is no thorough explanations for the memory of the immune system, if we take the precise meaning of (how) rather than referring to a few biochemical changes as an answer to the question.

The Genetics was fascinating too, even though this field of science by no means was as advanced as today. We now know much more. However, the function of 'DNA' and its relationship with messenger RNA and, the way that different proteins and other substances are laid down in the body seemed to me unbelievably delicate, regular and complex. Precise sequence of the nucleotides in each molecule of DNA is indeed unbelievable and what a major difference it makes, if only one of the units was missing or misplaced. The way that amino acids make the molecules of proteins and the role of 'mRNA' within the cells in such a process is amazingly fine-tuned and surely impossible to be an accidentally developed system and process. How genes, carry characteristics of the person to his offspring is equally startling and it becomes even more so when one appreciates that we have inherited some of the characteristics of ancestors who lived tens of thousands years ago.

The human brain with its complex structure and, with its delicate and mysterious functions is of an unbelievably sophisticated design. I strongly believed then, and still do, that capacity of human brain is far more than that of mere evolution, if one adheres strictly to the rules of Darwinism.

In Biology and Embryology, there were many more interesting points that fascinated me, and I only quote one example.   After the fertilisation (fusion of sperm and ovum) there is only a single cell (Zygote) that comprises one half of its genetic information from father and the other half from mother.   And then cell division begins leading to the inner group of cells (later to become embryo) and the outer group of cells (later to become protective membrane for the foetus). The embryo continues with the cell division and multiplication and then groups of the cells take on specific functions and roles.   From this stage onwards each cell (or group of cells) knows precisely which part or what organ of the body they are assigned to develop. They know exactly what their mission is. How do they know and in the healthy situations (when there are no interferences from infectious diseases or the chemicals), hardly ever make any mistake?   To me this was indeed a mystery and I thought it could not happen without the influence of another factor, another power.   Hundreds of physiological functions at cellular level that occupied my imaginations are beyond the scope, patience and place of this book. When I studied the biology and physiology of the human body in greater depth than I had at secondary school and when I contemplated on mysteries of the Immunology, Genetics and the central nervous system, I could no longer accept our conclusions with my intellectual friends; attributing everything to Darwin's theory of Evolution, Big Bang and merely to chances and accidents. I thought physiological and biological wonders in living creatures and especially in human beings was too sophisticated to be the result of accident or chance, too complex to be credibly explainable by mere natural selections and random genetic mutations. I thought delicacy of highly fine-tuned biological processes in the living things and complexity of their structures are beyond our simplistic assumption of spontaneous emergence. I found the splendours of life ineffable and any further insistence of scientists to attribute all of these to accident and chance seemed to me unbelievable indeed. Truly any more insistence to attribute all the regularities in nature to chance and accident could only be explained by; blindness resulting from one's arrogance, I thought. As for the capacity of human brain, this amazingly complex machine that had attracted my admiration more than anything else I asked this question. If in the process of evolution, nature selects the best traits for more survival, more reproduction, further development of the next generations and lastly for better adaptation with the changing environmental factors (as the theory of evolution tells us) then; why it was necessary to increase the capacity of our brain to this magnitudes when we were evolved from the apes? Natural selection could not have forced the process of the evolution to jump up by tens of steps from apes to humans because, changes are supposed to be gradual according to the same theory. Mutations causing the unexpected changes cannot produce such a refined structure either. Although they have not said so, as far as I know, even if scientists claimed that there was not only one but several missing links between apes and man, for which we have found no trace, the question would not and could not be answered. Because; in such a scenario we would have needed much bigger gaps between the arrival of apes and emergence of human beings; far more than what is assumed and we should surely have found some evidence for such a claim by now.

I have only referred to a few examples that, interested me in those days, but there is an ocean of fascinating facts in different fields of science. The more I learned and thought about the scientific discoveries and the extensive information scientists provided, the more I was convinced that what we see in human beings could not simply be the result or product of an accident or chance let alone the entire universe. Surely there must be a designer and creator. I came to a new conclusion since denying the existence of God at last meeting we had. And I began to observe nature with a totally different attitude and different eyes.

*

Everything in nature now seemed new to me as if I had not seen them before; so beautiful, complex, and sophisticated, so delicate and precise. Once again, I seriously thought about the twinkling stars and looked at the great spectacles of the starry heavens and, I remembered my intense feelings about them when I was a child. The heavens were as beautiful and as majestic as before if not more so. Stars took my mind to beyond the apparent scene, to the millions of galaxies, and to millions of stars or planets within each galaxy. I thought about the small part of the universe that we claim to know well and about the most part of which we know nothing at all. Then I appreciated the extent and scale of my ignorance. I regretted and was immensely ashamed of my arrogance (after rejecting God) when I must have had a temporary blindness not to have noticed the ineffable brilliance and grandeur of the creation. Planet Earth has a diameter of about thirteen thousand kilometres that may seem too big to us and indeed it is but it is only a tiny speck within our solar system. Our solar system measures fifteen million kilometres from one side to the other and yet such a system with its sun, planets and moons included is only a small part of our galaxy. Our galaxy is so huge that it would take more than hundred thousand years for light to travel from one end of it to the other and yet this is not the biggest galaxy, there are millions of them, some much bigger than ours and all astonishingly ordered with their planets and stars. In fact today scientists tell us that there are billions of galaxies and trillions of stars, planets and many other solar systems. They even talk about the possibility of there being other universes in the cosmos. How could any sensible and rational mind assume that all of these are accidentally or spontaneously made up entities? I really could not understand it; how could anyone deny the existence of a designer with so much evidence of design before them?

Of course, I did not reject the theories of Evolution or Big Bang; as neither I was nor I am in a position to do so. But I found it impossible to accept that the entire universe (with such a size and building blocks) and life (with such a sophistication and regularity) and, living creatures (with such a complex and fine-tuned structures) are only inadvertent products of a poorly explained explosion and evolution. I really thought, and believed, that something was missing in our calculations and debates. Recently, only few years ago (I do not remember whether I heard from radio or read it in newspaper) that a team of distinguished scientists after years of study and research concluded that humans were designed by designers who have (or had) higher intelligence and were (or are) living on one of the planets far away. What unbelievable stubbornness and arrogance of those atheists I said, it is indeed incredible. They have done magnificent work and with the scientific evidence have confirmed that there ought to have been a designer of man but rather than accepting God as the designer, they have returned to an old theory that suggests the existence of highly intelligent creatures somewhere in the universe who have designed us as an experiment. If human with comparatively inferior capabilities and intelligence (as those scientists imply), is so complex, sophisticated and fine-tuned that, they could not have been by-product of evolution, and needed designers to create him. Then, how on earth could any rational mind accept that those designers themselves, in a distant galaxy or planet, with much higher intelligence than human, came to existence without a designer or creator? Then I asked; is there any way to explain this mystery other than accepting the existence of God? Well, I had better leave that point for the moment and return to the narrative account of passages of the journey.

*

By this stage of journey, I had begun training in hospitals and therefore I was in closer contacts with the patients and their relatives. I saw suffering of the people on a daily basis and witnessed their tolerance, strength of their faith and their submission to the will of God. I experienced a great deal of happiness and satisfaction at being able to support patients, even though I was just a medical student. I found the faith (as well as the intelligence) of majority of the people respectful and by no means, naive and pitiful that I had earlier assumed to be the case. I could no longer look down on ordinary people and I didn't feel myself above them anymore. It appeared that arrogance was slowly leaving me and this, undoubtedly was another crucial factor for the change of heart and mind. Once the arrogance left me and once I truly experienced a totally different kind of happiness and satisfaction at the service of suffering patients I found readiness and time to listen to calls from inside that I had foolishly ignored for too long. For the first time I thought that I had found my inner self or at least I had vaguely become aware of her existence. Like most of people; for years my apparent self, had dominated and suppressed the inner self. I must admit that philosophers and psychologists have confused me by allocating different terminologies to the selves of humans. But in this book when

I refer to the inner (or real self, Devine self), I mean the self that talks to us from inside and, always expects and encourages the good thought and deeds. The self that loves other human beings and indeed all the living things, a self who has no doubt at all about the existence of God and is close to soul and conscience. Yes, in that period of journey I wondered whether the inner self was the same as soul and conscience but I was not sure yet.   All I knew was that she was there; right inside my being but with entirely different qualities.   However once I listened to my inner self, I could see the problem and shortcomings with conclusion of debates with the intellectuals; a conclusion that certainly was triggered or at least, was facilitated by my sadness and anger from the non-interference policy of God. Then I clearly saw the conditions that had led to the rejection of God specifically and religions at large.   At this point of my narrative I would like to refer to an old poem. I am aware of course, that it is difficult to translate a poem without destroying its beauty and the exact meaning of it. But I ought to refer to Hafez (mystic Persian poet of the fourteenth century), and before doing so, I should explain a couple of points which may take time but it is worth doing so. There is a myth about an ancient king of Persia called 'Jam' who had a magic cup (ball or globe) in which he could see everything and obtain all the news and information he required and get answers to his questions. They called it Cup of Jam (or Jameh Jam in Persian language). The other point to explain before translation of only one line of his poems is that, in the Persian poetry when they refer to the heart (Del, in Persian) they basically mean, where the desires, demands and emotions are felt. In poems it is indistinguishable from the self and mind. Now, Hafez says: "Salha, Del talab-eh Jam-eh Jam az ma mikard. Ancheh khod dasht, ze bighaneh tamanna mikard." Which literally means; "For years, heart eagerly was asking us, for the Cup of Jam. Ironically, what he already possessed, was begging from the stranger." I probably have ruined the poem of this great man but the point is that Hafez clearly refers to the inner self that has already (and indeed is) the Cup of Jam to see all the realities through it. If we find and free our inner self and empower it, we would certainly find the answers to mysteries too and like a magic mirror it would show everything.   Yes, it is true to say that I had become aware of my inner self at this stage of the journey but, when I look back, I realize that it was not yet a true awareness.   The combination of these factors persuaded me to revise our explanations in relation to the origin of universe and life, review the conclusions of our last meeting and justly ask this question. Is it honestly true that with the present knowledge we could confidently explain everything scientifically and no longer need God?

*

Coinciding with these changes in my beliefs and attitude there were also massive changes in the politics which were tragic indeed.   My friends were very upset and disappointed because, the Shah's regime had intensified the actions against freedom fighters. The secret police and intelligence service of the country (SAVAC) had become even more notorious, under direct influence, guidance and training of the CIA and MOSSAD and as a result, many young people had been killed and many more were imprisoned. They were not happy at all in general terms and my regression (as they called it) added to their misery. Clearly I too was saddened and disappointed. I remembered two previous defeats. The first one was an uprising by the nationalists and socialists (about twenty years before the time I'm narrating about) that was quashed by a CIA led coup to restore the Shah back to power after he fled the country. The second uprising (about ten years later) was mainly by a religious sector that was not only defeated but that defeat strengthened the Shah's ruling and his dictatorship. Years later of course, as readers would know, in 1979 these struggles finally led to one of the biggest revolutions in history. However, as a result of political set backs and restrictions and because I was very busy in hospitals and Medical School, my meetings with the infidels became less frequent. I therefore revised our conclusions almost alone and updated my friends whenever I could meet them. Revision began with the theory of Big Bang. Of course this theory has greatly advanced since then but, I refer to what we knew and understood of Big Bang in those days and, will return to that theory again later on. We were told that between ten to twenty billion years ago, nothing existed and then there was a high temperature gigantic explosion, which produced misty clouds and began expanding rapidly and cooling down, all the while. As it continued to expand and cool, the clouds of matter under the gravity came together to form denser and denser clouds from which; planets, stars and galaxies were born. In this version of the theory of Big Bang there were some unanswered questions that, I and perhaps the infidels, consciously or unconsciously had ignored. The thing that exploded probably was matter and if so, who created it? Where did energy of this magnitude to cause such an explosion come from? Obviously as I have said it before, I was not questioning the validity of this theory when thousands of respected scientists had already confirmed it. But these questions had not been properly addressed or answered, I thought.

As for the emergence of life, we were told that Planet Earth was created the same way as the other planets but, it remained in the right distance from the sun therefore, after billions of years there came the time that, our planet had the ideal conditions for the elements in water to join together and give birth to the first single cell living thing. And the rest is explained by the theory of evolution. From what I had learned in Biochemistry, Biology, Cytology and Genetics; this was simply impossible, logically as well as scientifically. There is no way that certain elements in water (or soup as they call it) could only by accident, without any plan and design by an outside power or designer, join together and go through the chemical reactions and per chance produce the highly complex and sophisticated molecule of the DNA, capable of duplication and reproduction. It is just unthinkable and impractical, I said. No scientist has ever been able to expound on this theory in the laboratory to show possibility of such a thing, not even a simple molecule, let alone a highly complex molecule of DNA, although they must have tried many times.   I could no longer agree with the conclusion of debates because it appeared that one had to accept too many coincidences to digest the reasoning.   That is to say; it just happened that there was plenty matter in space with the required elements in it and an unimaginable amount of energy inside it to explode. And it just happened that all the galaxies were formed in such meticulous order.   It just happened that, earth attained such a unique circumstances; favourable for life.   It just happened that the sun, essential for the life, was also there and the earth just happened to be in exactly the right distance from the sun to be neither too hot nor too cold. Finally, it just happened that a few elements in water accidentally joined together and went through a series of complex chemo-physical actions and reactions; to produce a highly elaborate and delicate structure of DNA. In fact not only I could not accept such assumptions, to explain the beginning of life, but I also believed that most scientists have already proved absurdity of their theory anyway. By that I mean; although most scientists particularly, at the early stages of their career are atheists (or more likely pretend to be so) ironically, with vast amount of information and knowledge that, they have made available to us; today believing in God is much easier than it was at the time of prophets. It is indeed interesting to note that nonbeliever scientists have helped the humans to fully appreciate greatness, majesty and glory of the creation and creator (unintentionally of course!) and they have done so, far more than anyone and anything else in the history of man. Indeed, it is for their ingenious discoveries and outstanding achievements that, we can see and perceive the impossibility of the birth of the universe and the beginning of life or emergence of humans on earth, to be purely accidental, without any design or purpose behind the creation. At this stage of the journey I realised that our knowledge of the realities in universe is so little that is almost nothing and specific subjects such as the birth of universe and beginning of life are not as simple as my intellectual friends, and most of the scientists for that matter, had thought it to be.

However, from what we know of the universe and life, even though negligible indeed, I came to conclusion that there must be a purpose for creation. And when one comes to believe in a creator it is only common sense to accept that the creator himself, must be uncreated otherwise there would be no end for the question of; who created him, her, this or that? The problem with me in that period was that I was trying to use conventional reasoning and rationalisation, to answer the questions, and so, I could not convince the atheist members of our society. I must confess that, even for the notion of design and purpose of creation (that I had assumed to be the case) I did not yet know what I meant by that. Having said it, I had a feeling that the purpose of man's creation could not be merely for the happiness attained from earthly pleasures that, my friends were indulging themselves generously and were saying, that is all why we are here for, no other purpose.

Chapter 6

There is no god but the God

It was in my final year of Medical School, that the Shah's notorious secret service and police had once again quelled the people's uprising and government banned all political activities. Indeed his strong army, police and intelligence services had virtually succeeded to terrorise, demoralise and silence everyone.   The brave and more serious activists had been either executed or murdered after barbaric torture and were buried in anonymous mass graves or were imprisoned while, (as it has always been the case) most of the leaders had escaped abroad.

Due to the escalation of the Shah's autocracy, where even social gatherings of friends or, any types of the meeting were banned I had more time for my education, training and also, for meditation on the spiritual aspects of life.   Of course, occasionally somehow I managed to see my friends too. By that time I had fully appreciated the shortfalls of the Big Bang theory to provide suitable answers to the question of the birth of universe and had seen the failure of most of theories, in explaining the origin of life and emergence of human through the evolution only. I honestly thought the theories were in need of evolution themselves and sincerely hoped that one day; science will give satisfactory answers to all the questions. Of course, I was a layman in such matters but even some scientists had objected to theories regarding the origin of life so another theory was produced. They said; life in the form of DNA came from another planet, when Earth was bombarded by a shower of meteorites and then this sample of life found favourable conditions in water and produced the first living thing; a cellule. .The arrival of DNA, or any living creature for that matter, aboard on extremely hot meteorite was equally unacceptable to me, indeed far more unlikely than their first version of their theory. How a poor living creature from another planet or few molecules of the DNA could have remained alive or undamaged to get here, if their vehicles were the meteorites of incredibly high temperature and with a speed of beyond the imagination; travelling for years?   With all respect to founders of the theory when I first heard about it I thought they were really joking. They cannot be serious I said. Could these scientists experimentally keep just one living creature of their own choice (alive) or merely one molecule of DNA (unspoiled) in comparable degree of heat and speed of travelling, not for years that meteorites had to make their journeys, but only for few hours?   Even if I could have accepted such an imaginary hypothesis the essence of question would have remained unanswered. I mean how did life begin in another planet before they decided to throw some DNAs, at Planet Earth?   Sending the question away to another planet or even to another galaxy; would not solve our problem nor could it answer it.   Although I it could take it out of sight and out of mind and someone else's problem!

135

In Searching God

*

I qualified from Medical School, spent eighteen months in compulsory military service worked for one year in rural areas as general practitioner and then, went to England for speciality training for five years and all this time I continued to be a fanatical reader; searching for the Truth and expecting to find it hidden somewhere inside books. I contemplated on the subjects as I read but more importantly I talked to (and listened to) my inner self and observed the majesty of nature carefully. I learned about God far more from Cup of Jam in my inner self, than from books. I learned far more from the study of nature than from debates with the intellectuals. I observed, acknowledged, appreciated and truthfully admired the meticulous, delicate and complex structure of everything in the nature that I managed to examine and consider and I saw the depth of their splendour and glory. I was indeed lucky that Medical School had taught (and trained) me to observe the subjects   scrupulously, to examine them thoroughly and methodically, visualise and imagine fascinating inner worlds of the subjects under examination, and not just their superficial or outward appearance. I had also learned how to use history, signs and symptoms of each patient to reach a correct diagnosis. So, using that technique I continued my search for the Truth with more hope than ever and it was indeed at this stage of the journey that I became fascinated and indeed thrilled to find out that nothing in nature is idle or motionless. I realised that everything in the universe as a whole and on Planet Earth, is definitely in motion, even a rock, a stone, wall or building, simply everything.   Within everything that one observes, considers and examines; there are constant movements, activities, birth, death and decay, renewals and a continuous exchange of energy.   There are endless changes and evolution, wherever you look and at whatever you find and examine.   Many things around us might appear still at the first glance but, in reality they are not still at all. There are fast and constant movements of the electrons in every single atom of them.   Inside everything there are numerous obvious or hidden chemical and physical actions and reactions that take place, all the time.   Truly, nothing in nature is the same at any given time compared with what it was just a second ago. So I realised and concluded that activities, movements and changes are inseparable parts and features of this planet if not the whole universe. I came to understand that creation is indeed continuous and evolution is the secret of creation as well as its destiny and clearly that applies to humans too.   Then I began to comprehend this notion more visibly and came closer to this belief that; development and evolution is man's destiny and fulfilling such a task is his mission on this planet.   This idea itself developed further and matured during the rest of journey that, I will discuss in more detail later in this book but here in the narrative, it is enough to add the following statements. I had already admired the structure, function and capabilities of the human brain but at this stage, I became even more conscious of the huge capacity of his brain and began to realise that; there must be a specific purpose behind the creation of such a dazzlingly complex machine, with such an amazing level of intelligence. I didn't think that the human brain and intelligence is solely to enable man to provide the necessities for his physical needs or respond to his animal desires. Clearly, it is too complex structurally, too great functionally and too high in its potential abilities to be for these purposes only. I thought that man and his brain is the masterpiece of creation not the stars that I had assumed to be God's masterpiece in that memorable summer, on top of the roof. Beside the undeniable splendour and wonders of the nature it was the human brain that had occupied my thoughts and had impressed me more than anything else. The human brain is a magnificent machine which can encompass the entire universe. But ironically, this amazing machine has not yet fully understood its own secrets and potential. Of course, today with the high technology, the scientists not only could detect but also interpret the electrochemical signals of neurones. By using electro-encephalography, computed tomography, magnetic resonance imaging and positron emission tomography and various other old or new means and instruments; scientists can now study the anatomy of the human brain and its numerous functions in details. And by these advances in the science and amazing technologies, they have certainly unravelled some of the secrets of the human brain but the vast majority of it remains a mystery. Indeed the human brain is the most fascinating but at the same time most difficult organ to study and discover its secrets. Here, there is a practical problem in using the brain (or any other machine) to study itself, to study its own structure, functions and secrets. Having said so, it seems that the scientists are getting there. The human brain contains a hundred billion cells (neurons) and the complexities of the interconnectivity between these cells by the synapses are well beyond any description. There are one million new connections between the neurons of brain per second of our life, really a powerful and hardworking machine. This amazing organ; has the power of imagination beyond the limit, ability of rationalisation and logic beyond any dispute and the gift of the memory beyond any doubt and yet regrettably, it lacks the ability to know and understand its own creator.   In spite of having such a powerful tool man has no immediate idea about the Truth, real knowledge or plan and purpose of creation.   Unless of course, one develops and elevates to much higher levels and that is an important matter to discuss later in this book. How could such a structure in our body be merely a servant on hedonistic life?

*

It was at this stage that, for the first time in my life, I fully appreciated and recognized that, not only there must be a God but also there ought to be a <u>mission </u>for man on this planet. Man could not be here accidentally nor could he be here simply to satisfy his physical desires or pursue an animalistic life; a type of life that does not need a brain with such magnitude that he possesses. Then I became convinced that God exists <u>which was nothing new</u>. It was the same conviction that I had when I was a child but this time it was for entirely different reasons. I came to this conclusion; <u>not</u> because my father had told me so, <u>not</u> because of the books, whether religious or philosophical, that I had read, <u>not</u> because of the religious and spiritual teachings that I had heard too often. I came to this conclusion; <u>not</u> because of a religious belief, <u>not</u> because of listening to countless debates and arguments between the atheists and theists that, I was involved for years and definitely <u>not</u> because of the fear of God or expecting a reward and favour from him whether in this or next world. I came to this conclusion because I appreciated the magnificence, glory and majesty of the universe that could not have come to existence accidentally. I came to this conclusion because of the complexities, delicacies and splendour of the creation as a whole, because of the breath- taking grandeur and beauty of nature and because of the human brain; this masterpiece of creation. And above anything else I came to this conclusion because of the intuitive mind and evidence of inner self and revelations of the magic mirror inside.

Having reached this point on journey once again I thought that although realistically it is not possible to define God but if by referring to him we mean the being who has created the entire world and himself is uncreated then by such a working definition one would conclude that there could only be one God. Regarding this point I had no problem with the attitudes of the atheists and infidels as I could appreciate that they simply do not believe in God (whether he is one or more) but I wondered why on earth theists and religious people would not acknowledge such an obvious fact, or do they? I thought by this comprehension and reasoning there could not be more than one Truth and one God. So, it is entirely wrong for any person to proclaim; God of Israel, God of Christians, God of this God of that, because in all religions and faiths God must be (and indeed is) the same.   Innocently and rather optimistically, I wished that if only everyone could accept this principal fact then all the unfortunate conflicts, blind hatreds and old hostilities amongst religions and their believers could be resolved.   A dear friend of us (a pleasant Christian lady), sends us Christmas card every year and, never forgets to add, "May your God and my God bless you". Poor lady, she thinks every single religion should have its own God and sadly she is not the only one. The reality is that majority of the faithful believers of religions have been brought up with such belief and understanding.   In talking about this serious matter with a friend of mine he said, "You're right.   There could only be one God but sadly everyone assumes his or her God is the true God, and this also applies to idolaters; they too believe that their hand made god is true God." I'm afraid I had to face with this unfortunate and sad reality that began from ancient religions and continued to present day.   The problem is that, people have always had a desire and feeling, to give a specific name, character and image to their (god) rather than to accept the concept of an invisible God; who is unknowable, indefinable and mysterious to us. This lack of appreciation and acceptance is in my view, perhaps the root and cause of majority of all sorts of problems and conflicts on this planet.

However, I became familiar with views of the Sufi Mystics of Islam that, God could not be seen or described unless one spiritually develops and elevates to the highest levels and become a perfect human, in order to be at the presence of God. And this is a prestige that, possibly very few humans like Jesus Christ and the Prophet Mohammad have attained. About eight hundred years ago Saadi a Persian poet said, "Man can reach the levels that sees nothing but the God." And that is the essence of teaching of any true religion as far as I can understand providing of course, the teachings were not altered or degraded. At this stage, I also firmly believed that the existence of God could only be understood and accepted; by appreciation of the majesty and glory of the entire creation that, any rational and just mind would willingly accept that, it could not have come to being without a creator. I believed God is not a hypothesis to be proved experimentally, even though if one wishes to pursue his search solely through that line; today there is ample scientific evidence for his purpose. I was further convinced that one ought to find and free his inner self from the prison of his false self and empower her in order to see the reality through the existing inside mirror and value his own intuitive mind. It is sad to say that we often forget the gifts within us and beg for science to provide answers to mysteries, show us the Truth and teach us the real Knowledge. Albert Einstein once said, "The intuitive mind is a sacred gift and the rational mind a faithful servant. We have created a society that honours the servant and has forgotten the gift." That is right, we have forgotten the gift.

*

Non-believer scientists might refuse to accept anything that is invisible or the hypothesis of its existence has no solid scientific evidence and cannot be proved experimentally. In their opinion such criteria, applies to God too. Interestingly at the same time they confess that denying the existence of God is not possible. Like most people I too can understand and accept the irrefutability of God's existence, but I would not agree with the agnostic view of the infidels that God's existence could not be proved either. In fact I believe that his existence can be proved, but not by orthodox scientific methods, observation and applied experiment in laboratory if that is what the atheists mean and want. However, I find their arguments illogical. For example, the condition of visibility as a rule for accepting a fact is quite amusing. Does it mean that billions of bacteria, virus or any other tiny things that before the invention of microscope could not be seen, did not exist in

147

the past?   Could we honestly deny the existence of our own thoughts, imaginations, conscience, feelings and emotion just because we cannot see them? I did not think so.   If something is invisible to us, either because of its nature or, because we have not yet found the means and skills to observe; does not mean that, it does not exist.   It simply means that we have not yet developed or equipped adequately to see the reality.   As for the scientific evidence to prove the existence of God, as I mentioned earlier, I thought that our scientists have already found enough evidence and proved it beyond the doubt. All we need to do now is to appreciate and observe them considerately, to examine them patiently and, contemplate on gigantic amount of new discoveries and information, in order to recognize and admit the presence of design in every single thing and in every corner of the universe.   Having done so, we will certainly accept the existence of the designer, which mankind has called God.   It seems that at this period of the spiritual journey, I had begun to acquire preliminary concept or a glimpse of understanding of mystical views but that is for later in the book. When I arrived at this phase I thought I should seriously revisit my doubts and uncertainties which had caused so much anguish for me.   In case my past judgments were reckless, once again to look at the ancient and new scriptures that we had so carelessly ridiculed and criticised and review my views and understandings of true religions that my intellectual friends and I had dismissed off hand so impolitely. I thought I should reassess new versions of the theories (in relation to the birth of the universe and the origin of life) and finally find out what remained from doubts and questions that I had.   Do I still stand by my anger and foolish criticism of God regarding his attitude of inertia towards the atrocities throughout the world or to the injustices and inequalities in human societies?   I believed it was right time to revise my views and I began to do so as carefully as I could and put the result to the intellectuals of café Naderi whenever I could meet them in spite of the restrictions that autocrats had imposed upon the nation.

Chapter 7

Scriptures and religions

When I had clarified my thoughts, once again believed in the creator (and hoped this would be a lasting conviction), I returned to the difficulties that I had with sacred books, to revisit my criticism of their contents. I also reviewed the doubts and uncertainties that philosophical and religious books caused me. I contemplated on the questions and objections that I had raised against God, when I was young, but this time with an entirely different attitude. By this time I had returned from England, had established my private practice and had been appointed as academic member in a Medical School. The Resistance to the Shah's regime had intensified and a guerrilla type of struggle was spreading very fast. I found the few remaining intellectuals of Café Naderi, new members among them. Once again; being at the service of patients whom I was able to help more as a specialist, witnessing the extent of their sufferings, recognizing the extent of their tolerance and appreciating their genuine humility and sense of gratitude; provided me with invaluable opportunities to become aware of things I had not noticed before. At the same time as I was teaching medical students, their motivating queries and comments challenged me to look more seriously at matters. I learned a great deal from both groups.

*

However, as for the sacred books especially ancient scriptures, I thought to do justice and to be realistic; one ought to consider the time and circumstances in which the content of these books were spoken, remembered or recorded and years later compiled into a book. One ought to study the history behind every one of such books before passing any comment or judgement. I asked myself, what should one really expect from the content of these sacred books, if the teaching materials and stories within them were expressed sometime between two to five thousand years ago, by a language and style suitable to the understanding and acceptance of the primitive people of those eras when most of them were certainly illiterate and with all respect to our ancestors, relatively uncivilised?   What should one expect if at the time, when stories were told and later on, when they were written in books the technology, information and scientific knowledge were extremely restricted?   Indeed, how different these books would have been if the prophets, priests, philosophers and scribes had access to the skill, technology, information, scientific discoveries and knowledge of today?   What should one expect from these books if the subject matter (after passing by word of mouth for many years) with all the likely corruption, alterations, omissions and additions and more significantly misinterpretations; were eventually written down at least partly for the sake of protecting the interests of priests or rulers, if not entirely for that purpose?   What percentage of the accuracy and rationality one could find in these books, if they have been subject to many genuine and deliberate mistranslations, censorship and extensive editorial alterations by scribes, priests or those in power before reaching us? We can dismiss the content of the Old Testament that is surely expected to be affected by the above mentioned factors anyway, bearing in mind the very long time it took before the compilation, but what about the New Testament? How many times was the book subject to similar changes and censorship? How many centuries passed by before the priests and politicians allowed the general public to have access to the already altered and edited versions of the New Testament? How many copies of translated ones from the Greek or Hebrew that were smuggled to England (and other countries), were burnt by the Christian priests in order to compel the ordinary believer to read or listen to Latin version of the book, understand not a single word of it and therefore, accept whatever the cardinals, bishops and priests tell or interpret for them?　　How many people were burnt alive; for simply possessing and reading the New Testament in native languages?　　There has been much research (regarding the history of Old and New Testaments) that confirm numerous deliberate or genuine mistakes in translation from the Greek and Hebrew originals to other languages as well as many add-ons from the corrupted rabbis and priests, before reaching to ordinary people. I've no doubt that the same applies to other religious books to a lesser or greater extent. One has to acknowledge that, in these books apart from all misunderstandings and mistakes in translation, there have been so much material imposed on, through the years that, much of the original words have been lost as a result of malicious editing and selfish additions and alterations. Therefore, critical analysis of every subject matter and every single word or sentence in them; seems inappropriate. In a debate about God, referring to matters written in sacred books and based on them denying his existence (a tactic regularly used by atheists) is obviously inappropriate, illogical and indeed, wholly unjustified too. I thought that it would be very helpful if the leaders and the scholars of all religions could get together; in order to identify, separate and discard all the irrational and disgraceful parts of the scriptures but I knew that, they would never do such a thing, because it is not in their interests to rock the boat or put their empires in danger. In most debates about God's existence, apart from this routine question of; "if there should be a creator for everything then, who created God?" infidels typically have two more main weapons to argue. One is referring to the content of scriptures and the other is lack of scientific evidence to support his existence. If you take away the books, there will be very little left for them to argue. Because as I mentioned before; ironically by their own magnificent findings, particularly by astronomical discoveries, showing the grandeur of the universe, and by physiological, biological and other scientific information that have been made available; the scientists have already paved the way for any

156

rational person to conclude that God ought to exist. However, in spite of all the inevitable and expected nonsense, ridiculous stories and loads of garbage that I had found in some of these sacred books, when I referred to them again (this time unbiased I hoped) I discovered many philosophical and spiritual teachings in them too, as well as many moral points. I thought that we had undoubtedly exaggerated the nonsense in these books and had not seen or appreciated vast amount of spiritual and moral subjects in them and if we had noticed any, we had not taken them seriously.   But in spite of acknowledging these points I continued to believe that in meditations about God (and in debates related to his existence) one must put the ancient scriptures aside. And if it was really necessary to refer to content of them (or any other sacred book) one ought to consider solely the parts that make sense and are consistent with the essence of the original doctrines.   Defending every single word written in the sacred books is waste of time and perhaps because of the extent of corruption in them inappropriate too, but I thought that some of the subjects that are frequently referred to and ridiculed by the infidels could be explained; of course for the sake of arguments with my intellectual friends and certainly not so seriously.

For example, when one reads that God created human from dust or clay it refers to the fact that human's body contains exactly the same elements that clay does; that are carbon, hydrogen, oxygen, nitrogen, calcium, iron and other major and minor elements. It suggests humility and intends to prevent and eliminate arrogance and selfishness, by reminding us that; as far as building blocks of living things as a whole and human specifically are concerned, there is not much difference between the human, animals and clay because we are all made from the same elements. As a matter of fact today top astronomers are telling the similar thing. They say, "We are all star dusts". Having said so, it is crucially important to acknowledge that, although in only analysis of our physical existence, we have nothing more than the clay or animals but when you consider things beyond the physical side there is indeed a huge difference that, second part of the same statement addresses. When it goes on to say that God breathed (or blew) into the image of man, it refers to the inner self, soul, intuitive mind and conscience that are God's gifts and this is the huge difference that, I mentioned earlier. Of course, there will be no difference between the humans, animals, plants and inanimate objects, if one lets his false-self free to dominate the real self by its animal nature and demands and therefore, shape purely a materialistic life to keep him in an animal stage. About creating everything in six days one could argue that the authors of such statement meant it in an entirely different scale. In other words billions of years might be like six days in the case of God, if at all time is applicable to him and his works in the first place. Having said so (as I mentioned before) I personally believe that the creation is not over and surly it continues. As for God's resting on the seventh day, one can assume that, inventors of such statement wished to persuade the people; to have planned and regular rest from their work and occupation (that today we accept as a necessity for the people's physical and mental health) but of course, they chose a bizarre way to persuade them.   It is obvious that, God does not need to rest and not all the religions have referred to such thing.   Having briefly attempted to defend or interpret a few examples from the sacred books I believe that, (bearing in mind the time and circumstances in which these scriptures have been written) there is certainly no logic in defending and justifying every single matter written in them and one should be fair and only judge them objectively and within their own limits.

As for the religions, that the intellectuals had ridiculed and dismissed out of hand and I too had my doubts and reservations; in revising my thoughts I arrived at an entirely different view. I do not address the following few sentences to those who do not accept God in the first place let alone to acknowledge his messengers, prophets and their established religions. But if we believe in the existence of God and accept that he created the entire universe and human beings with a plan and purpose then, we ought to also accept that he would assist us in variety of ways so that, we recognise our mission on earth and make an effort to achieve our goals. Precious help is already provided; via the human brain (with its massive capacity to observe, think, imagine and rationalise), his Divine self (in my opinion a direct connection to God) and his intuitive mind (this sacred gift). We can of course, do a great deal with these gifts; to understand nature, search for the Truth and achieve personal development and spiritual elevation. But we are also helped by the ingeniousness of the theoreticians, philosophers and scientists, whose brains have the capacity well beyond the norms. Equally; it is a reality that humans have been guided by the prophets who perhaps, from being ordinary persons; developed, evolved and reached

161

highest spiritual levels and then, through inspiration and Divine revelation acquired real knowledge.   And then they tried to enlighten the people with their doctrines, later on to be known as their religions. Why could this not be the case I asked my friends?   Why not accept that, just as the philosophers and scientists who helped their fellow human beings to advance; prophets also did the same?   Prophets were the inspired philosophers and the social scientists of their own era.   Truly, I could not find any difference (in principle of course) between the reality of existence of numerous philosophers and scientists throughout the history, and their massive influences in shaping human societies, with the comparable possibility of emergence of the prophets and their contributions.   Philosophers established schools of thought just as prophets established their religions and both contributed to human progress and development. In the past, when humans were not yet advanced in sciences, prophets emerged to explain splendour of creation to people, in a non-scientific language stressing spiritual and moral matters in life, by using the supernatural explanations. They did so to teach the people that God exists and show them the requirement of having faith and rule of law in the human societies. They tried to make the people recognise their mission for self- development. Today it is the scientists and philosophers who are in the front line with an identical task. Whether conscious or not; today scientists are helping human beings to climb the ladder towards perfection. They do this by digging out the information buried and hidden in the nature, by unravelling the mysteries of the universe and by showing the grandeur of the creation and the glorious greatness of the creator, in an entirely different ways, appropriate to our times. I believe that even those scientists who work hard to prove that, the universe and humans came to existence accidentally, inwardly confess that, it is in fact their own research, own findings and information which prove otherwise but I might be wrong.

However, the prophets led the human race forward and religions made indisputable contribution to the attainment of man. The majority of the greatest works of art, literature, poetry, music, paintings and sculpture, have been created by the inspirations from and for the love of God. I've no doubt that without the influence of religions; these invaluable treasures that are in the possession of human societies would not have been in such richness. Likewise the influence and contributions of the scientists and philosophers in progress and development of the humans are beyond any disputes and we owe enormous gratitude to both sides. My infidel friends were wrong to write off religions so lightly. I thought their attitude and judgement was partly influenced by their hatred of religious corruption and by ludicrous rituals and superstitions that had been added to them. I wonder whether their views were influenced by their political convictions. Sadly in dark days of history; Christian religious leaders burnt scientists alive in unbelievably cruel ways or, kept them in dungeons for years to die in dreadful conditions.   On the other hand, scientists were so angry that theologians persisted with superstitions, ceremonies and rituals that, they rejected all religions and God (a tit-for-tat situation). They rejected God because the idea did not stand up to their scientific scrutiny, and in so doing; strictly confined their efforts to materialistic science. Today, there is no such division between the scientists and religious leaders or, is that my dream?

One of the intellectuals' arguments was that if there is only one God then why has he sent so many different prophets with different religions, laws and guidance?   As a matter of fact in returning to the religious sources I realised that, if one really concentrates on the spiritual and moral aspects of the main religions one would certainly appreciate that, vast amount of their teachings are in relation to virtue and becoming good people.   And more importantly, if one could ignore the corrupted side of main religions and disregard the added superstitions and rituals, he would admit that there is in fact a remarkable similarity amongst them. In my opinion the essence of teachings in all higher religions is almost the same, bearing in mind the fact that, they have been addressed to different people in different periods of human's history and in a language and style suitable for that period.   What make them so different are the added and edited parts, the rituals, ceremonies and dogmatism about trivial matters.   The fact is that in all true religions their fundamental aim is to teach and guide people; so that they could develop and acquire good characters, to help them to progress and have respect for moral values.   Their ultimate task is to free mankind from his base animal nature and attain higher spiritual levels. This is certainly true, when you exclude the additions and study the core of doctrines of religions, from Hinduism to Islam. I came to conclusion that, if we merely consider matters such as virtue and self-development any differences that we might notice would be the manner that each religion presents. I thought most of the philosophical, spiritual and moral matters within the doctrines are essentially the same and only when it comes to the superstitious ceremonies and rituals they seem totally different religions.   More strikingly when one independently compares the original teachings of two universal religions (Christianity and Islam), providing one discards the inaccurate parts; similarity becomes even more obvious except for the difference of opinion regarding the nature of Jesus Christ.   I wish that all Moslems could read the teachings of Jesus Christ and all Christians could read the correct translation of The Quran in order to appreciate the point that I make and appreciate the striking similarities of philosophical, moral and spiritual matters in them.   In fact right from the start, if such awareness was possible and if the people had accepted that there is only one God for the whole universe and there is no major differences between religions; we would have had neither the shameful crusades, or similar atrocities in distant past, nor we would have witnessed new versions of such crimes at present time.

True religions are constructive and, contrary to what the infidels claim, they do not bring passivity. I believe we could neither have progressed to this level, nor enjoy today's civilisation; were it not for the influence of religions. Sadly, in spite of my opinion regarding the similarity between the higher religions (in their purest forms), I had to agree with the intellectuals of Cafe Naderi and accept this unpleasant reality that; in their existing forms, there are in fact deep differences between the main religions, alongside the old wounds, cruel hostilities, hatred and violent conflicts. And those in power will not do anything to resolve it. The intellectuals on the left of political spectrum took this point seriously and said, "Most if not all of the ancient and modern differences, hatreds and conflicts will continue, because the big powers need them too. They need it to create the terror and then with the excuse of fighting with the terrorism; terrorise people with wars, mass murders and destruction. Major Powers desperately need all these in order to achieve their objectives, least of which is arms sale. It is a bitter fact that they must rip off weaker nations in order to maintain prosperity of their own lands, their own luxurious lives and welfare of their own people. And this could only be achieved when there is the rule of jungle on earth that is to say, "powerful is always right and takes all at the cost of misery and suffering of the weak". I had to admit what they said. Big powers' demand could not be possible in a peaceful world and in virtuous societies. They could not achieve their objectives if there was brotherhood and sisterhood among the nations. And I had to also admit that, for the big powers maintaining the difference between the religions is the most efficient weapon to create the required hostilities amongst the nations, and achieve their purpose. So I asked myself; how we could expect them to resolve the differences.

In Searching God

*

Christianity and Islam, in their original and uncorrupted forms (if not most of religions) support the weak, oppressed and the men and women who are in need of help. Both religions condemn inequality and social injustice, and both of them invite the people to embrace brotherhood, righteousness and charity.   Both Jesus Christ and Prophet Mohammad strongly opposed poverty and the accumulation of the wealth for the few.   Their true followers also rose against the inequalities in human societies in their own time and struggled for social justice. Even today, when true Christian or Moslem priests preach along those lines and defend the poor and oppressed ones in societies, they are labelled as political socialists.   Indeed, true religions have always defended the poor, the weak and the oppressed and therefore, I was wondering, how my dear revolutionary friends and I, had not appreciated this aspect of the religions?   Some people have said that Ali (son in law of Prophet Mohammad) was the first socialist of recorded and known history. Having carefully studied his life and, having read his letters and commandments to the officials of his time and text of his speeches I can see why they say this. Yes, if being against inequality, opposing oppression within human societies, struggling to provide and maintain the social justice and defending rights of the weak, poor and those in need, is what is meant by socialism, then Ali definitely was a socialist except that, not the first one in written history but second to Jesus Christ. It was not surprising to see that, this statement delighted my atheist friends. However, not only do major powers and politicians not wish to see the end of conflicts between various religions but also influential religious leaders do not attempt to resolve differences either, nor will they ever give up rites and ceremonies. They neither would fight with the superstitions nor would they ever teach the followers that there is only one God and all the religions are essentially conveying the same principles. "No, they would not do so." I murmured, "Simply because they don't wish to lose their empires." My frustrated friends once again repeated their borrowed idea by declaring that, "Whatever they do and whatever you dream of, practically all the religions are the opium of nations that make them submissive and obstruct their progress". I am afraid they were absolutely right if people are only taught about the rituals and ceremonies, if they are encouraged to believe the superstitious garbage and, if they are merely concerned about gifts and sacrifices or, if they worship relics, pictures and statues of manufactured saints. But my infidel friends would have been absolutely wrong if people were taught about the philosophical, spiritual and moral aspects of true religions and, if they were taught and led on the path to righteousness and acquire good characters and finally, if they were led to worship only one invisible God and nothing or nobody else.

At this stage, I had come to a firm belief that the worship of another human, (whatever is the status and whether alive or dead) is returning to idolatry and from theistic point of view is blasphemous and I subscribe to this view even today. Not only is such worship wrong but I also believe that, bowing or prostrating oneself before another human is totally wrong and disgraceful and indeed against the dignity of man. Human beings should only bow to unseen God and no one else, whatever is the position of that person. Of course, we must respect the religious leaders or those men and women who spiritually have developed and elevated to higher levels, but this should not proceed to worshipping. Even worshipping of God, ought to be understood that, this is only for our own sakes, for our own developments and spiritual elevations. God neither needs our prayers and worship, nor is he in need of receiving any sacrifice or gift to grant us his love and protection.

In Searching God

While revising my thoughts about religions; I noticed another sad and bitter fact. In reality human beings are prone to do wrong and commit crime and that is why in modern societies we have the governments, police and laws to prevent such things. I believe religions did exactly that, and still do, and indeed do it far better than the man made laws. Of course, some people would never do wrong nor commit any immoral deeds whether or not there is any law to prevent them and whether or not they believe in any religion or God. They do not commit any offence simply because they are righteous and of good character. But the bitter reality is that, the rest of the people would avoid committing the unlawful deeds simply because of their fear of law and punishments and if they are religious persons, also because of their fear of God. In fact in practical terms, fear of God is more likely to prevent the unlawful deeds and crimes in this latter group of people, as they know that God is everywhere all the time and sees everything, whereas the eyes of law may not always be

174

watching. Therefore, in lawless and wild societies of older days, prophets had no option but to frighten the people with the wrath of God, in order to keep uncivilised people orderly and to prevent crime and chaos. The intellectuals and I should have appreciated that, Moses' and later on, Quran's insistence on this point was appropriate for certain era. We should not have criticised this nor see it as the weakness of religions. As a matter of fact without the law and without the fear of God, no one would have been safe in societies of the distant past and the rule of jungle or worse would have dominated daily lives. Of course, in an ideal world fear of punishment, whether by God or law, should not be the reason for righteousness, virtues, good deeds or good thoughts but sadly we are not living in ideal world. Talking about the fear of God, it should be noted that to be a righteous person only in the hope of reward (in this or the next world) or because of the fear of God's wrath; might be good enough and acceptable at certain elementary stages of personal development and spiritual evolution, when the higher motives are not yet intelligible. At this stage of development, a fear of God is understandable and indeed useful for the individual, as well as his community. But as the personal relationship with God evolves and advances, as one develops further and higher spiritual levels are attained; the nature of the fear changes too. The fear of God at the elementary stages is purely fear of his wrath and punishment but at higher levels of development it is only (love) and (the fear) if there is any, is only the fear of being deprived of God's love or not to have attained the merits of loving him.

However, history shows that man has committed many disgraceful and unbelievable crimes and has acted far worse than wild animals. I have no doubt at all that if it were not for the influence of religions that invite the people to act in good faith and if it was not for the fear of God's wrath; the history books would have been saturated by even worse crimes and by far more atrocities than have been recorded. This is true even though we must confess that some of the worst crimes were in fact committed at the instruction of the religious leaders. I do not imply that religious people would not commit crimes or act unlawfully and immorally, far from it. There are many religious people and even religious leaders who commit more offences and crimes than the non-religious ones and we have all seen and heard about them. I might be wrong of course, but I honestly believe that these religious criminals, (if such a label could be applied to them!) are not truly religious people and only pretend to be. The fact is that those groups of criminals do not believe in anything like that, and if they are truthfully religious people and believe in God then, we have to conclude that they have failed to develop and they are still enslaved by their false selves, their animal instinct and desires or demands. There are many priests and theologians amongst us, who are by far more dangerous to humanity than atheists. On the other hand there are many atheists and non-believers who are truly perfect examples of good humans and indeed, role models for those who seek righteousness. I've met and known many humanists, socialists and communists who were far more humane and virtuous than most priests and yet they did not believe in God. Being religious does not guaranty his righteousness. But on the whole the likelihood of a theist person (or a community) to practice virtues and justice, to observe the humanity and moral values and avoid crime; is far greater than that of an atheist or a community without religion. This is a reality and we need only refer to history books to acknowledge; excellent examples of the human societies in the early years of Buddhism and in early decades of Christianity and Islam; to fully appreciate the practice of virtue and the creativity of the people in those eras. Surly, this was the case and reality, until first the religious leaders and then, their followers, were corrupted and had distanced themselves from their original doctrines. I have no doubt at all that if certain political and religious leaders in those darkest periods of history were truly theists and religious the atrocities, crimes and cruelties against the humanity, would not have happened. Indeed, it is very sad to see that in the name of God and religions; tyrants have justified their actions and they will continue to do so for generations to come.   Contrary to the opinions of my intellectual friends, in reviewing my thoughts about the religions, I concluded that; as long as religions make the people better persons and teach them morality and virtue, it is definitely good for the human societies and it is undeniably an excellent means of self-development and spiritual elevation. This conclusion is valid even if the religions were man-made and had nothing to do with God. However, in that stage of journey I began to respect all religions and I thought it mattered not which religion one believes at and practices, as long as one knows and acknowledges that, there is only one God for the entire universe and not one God for each religion. It does not matter which religion, as long as one can distance oneself from superstitions, ancient or new rituals or ceremonies and as long as one does not worship anything or anyone else except for God. And finally, as long as one knows that worshiping is for his own development and it is not a favour to God or for the purpose of purchasing the celestial rewards.

Chapter 8

The universe and life

Shortly before I rejected the existence of God and, was officially honoured to be a full member of the society of atheists; we had arrogantly concluded that the theories of Big Bang and Evolution explain everything. But in the light of my recent change of heart and mind, the fundamental questions regarding the birth of universe and the origin of life required revision. Since that period of my life, scientists have produced various modified versions of the old theories and have presented the new ones which alongside the fresh discoveries have led to heated debates. Every time scientists declared a different version of the old theories I saw that; whatever the new discoveries and information and whatever the formats of the revised theories and whatever the astronomers do with energy or matter (in order to explain the birth of universe and origin of the life more acceptably) the inevitable reality is that; those fundamental questions remain unchanged and un-answered. My scientist friends were very annoyed and indeed hated to hear me repeat my simple questions after I had politely listened to their exciting news about the universe and life.

If they had said, "Precisely twelve billion years ago, just before the gigantic explosion of Big Bang the entire matter of universe was condensed in one place as small as a baseball or, as small as head of a pin and the space was confined to small area around the condensed matter." I would merely show my intense surprise of such a probability and gently ask; where did that matter come from in the first place? And who managed to condense the entire matter of the universe (as we comprehend it today) to as small as a ball or tip of a pin? No need to say that I would not hear a convincing reply and therefore, the inquiry would roll over to be repeated following the subsequent new discovery and the explanations. So, you can see why they were so irritated.   Those pleasant meetings that I had with my scientist friends are clearly still in my mind and I would like to narrate them, as if they were happening right now.

They talk about topics such as quantum physics, production of the matter and subatomic particles after Big Bang and cosmic background radiation as signature of heat resulting from the gigantic explosion. Then, when they notice that I do not quite understand what is meant by quantum physics and what is the nature of energy in the first place, they look at me pitifully and wonder how have I managed to become a doctor with such a poor level of the intelligence?   For a few minutes they would enjoy their superiority but then with another simple question arising from common sense, for that they have no answer, they would get irritated again. When they declare that, as a matter of fact there was no matter to begin with; it was only energy that caused gigantic explosion of Big Bang and created the matter. I look at them with obvious surprise and show my thirst and enthusiasm to hear more, purposely, delaying the repetition of question for the time being. They continue to explain further, to make sure that I could understand the new theory by stating that Einstein's equation of E=mc2 arising from his special theory of relativity, plainly tells that energy is equivalent to matter multiplied by the speed of light squared.   This simply means that energy and matter are interchangeable and so following the Big Bang the force of inflation converted the original energy to matter, and then, as the cloud of newly produced matter was escaping from the centre of explosion, space was also expanded.   Thereafter, the matter spread incredibly fast into the newly expanded space and formed all these stars and planets within the galaxies. "To begin with," scientists try to make it easier for me to understand, "all matter was in the form of immeasurable number of subatomic particles (practically impossible to observe, measure or weigh) that randomly collided with each other, fused and created 'hydrogen' as the smallest atom to

184

begin with and then 'helium' and other elements of the matter that we have on Planet Earth and perhaps in other planets and stars of galaxies as well." I am stunned to hear all this and am truly speechless and so they continue with their explanation, "The universe comprises over a hundred billion galaxies that on average are about one million light years apart." They go on lecturing, "And within each galaxy, there are billions of stars and planets all originating from the same subatomic particles that came to existence following the explosion and conversion of the energy". They pour out more new information. I learn that the universe that we are talking about has an ineffable size and weight that is impossible to visualise, let alone to measure or weigh, and yet, such an unimaginable and incomprehensible size and weight only applies to visible chunk of the universe. The astronomers have begun to believe that there might be much more in the universe that we have not discovered yet and there might be even other universes in cosmos. Honestly, I am overwhelmed with all of the information. I hear them alright and try hard to imagine the size of the universe and the amount of matter and energy in it but obviously I cannot and to tell the truth; my mind is somewhere else as they continue to talk. "The sun moves at speed of a million miles per hour," I can hear them explaining; "and it takes almost two hundred million years to go round our galaxy once. And yet this galaxy among the billions of other galaxies is not the biggest one at all. The visible universe is so huge that, some of the galaxies lie eleven million light years away from us." At this point of their lecture, they decide to inform me that, the speed of light is one hundred eighty six thousand miles per second, in case I do not know. No, I can't take it any more of their lecture. I can't visualise nor comprehend the vastness of the immeasurable universe but I can definitely appreciate its splendours and admire complex and fine-tuned structure and order of the entire creation and that is where my mind is, while the intellectual pour out their new information so enthusiastically. I'm truly relieved to learn from the scientists that it is not only I, who cannot comprehend and visualise the vastness of the universe; even some of the ingenious, respected and famous astronomers believe that, universe is massive beyond all of the expectations, beyond all of our imaginations and it extends well beyond the eleven billion light years span of the strongest telescope available today. They believe that vastness of the universe (or universes!) may reach infinity. Being pleasantly puzzled and astonished to hear all their new information and discoveries I look at them with wonder as well as with utmost delight, love, regard and satisfaction. I do so, not only because I see that my sceptic friends describe the greatness of creation and creator so beautifully and so skilfully (obviously, with no intention to do any favour to theists) but also; because I witness the extent of the capability, capacity and function of the human brain that I had declared to be the masterpiece of creation, although the stars were still most beautiful things and very close to my heart. I think about the energy and say inside; "They use this word so confidently as if they really know what it is."

Then, not being an astronomer or scientist at any of the related

fields, I cautiously ask, "Is it not true that energy might change

from one form to other (if the theory is correct in practice) but

never vanishes? So, following the Big Bang; if some portion

of the energy was converted to matter and created all of the

galaxies, is it not true to say that we ought to be able to

visualise or guess the greatness of that initial energy utilised

for such a conversion, using the same formula of Einstein but

from the other end? Obviously we cannot weigh the stars and

planets of billions of galaxies, but we can try to imagine the

amount of energy which could be produced if all the matter in

universe was converted back to initial energy (which would be

exactly the same amount of energy that was used to create the

matter in the first place following the gigantic explosion).

Where did such an ineffable amount of energy come from?

The amount of energy that; not only some of it was converted

to matter in the universe but enough was left, to make life

possible. What is the energy in the first place and how did it come into existence"? They do not know the answer. The fact is that, whether one takes the matter first and suggests that entire matter of today's universe was condensed in one place as small as a baseball or, one takes the energy first and claims that, somehow this puzzling thing exploded and was converted to matter the question would remain the same; where did they come from? Indeed it makes no difference either how small were those particles of pre-matter, (if I may call them so) because their total mass and weight ought to be exactly the same as of all the galaxies today. Truly that ought to be the case, if we are suggesting this was how the matter came to the existence in the first place? And that was how the galaxies were made? Yes, those heated discussions remain in my mind but let us return to former style of narration. I thought my atheist friends had every right to hate these questions simply because if they had said that matter or energy already existed (without being created), they would have lost an important weapon in their arguments against the existence of God. Because, in all of our debates they kept asking me; who has created your God? And they categorically rejected any possibility of his existence, without being created. In other words by accepting such a possibility (that energy or matter already existed without being created) they also had to accept the possibility of God's existence, uncreated. On the other hand, if they had accepted that, matter or energy was created before the gigantic explosion occurred, then they had to also accept the existence of creator that human has named God. However, in my view, today science leads us to confidently believe in God but arrogance does not permit some of us, to accept this reality. That being said, I find it remarkable that some of the astronomers and famous scientists have used the word primordial which basically means existing from the beginning (in other words uncreated). In their articles and books you can see them referring to a primordial atom (or mass), when they talk about the birth of universe or referring to a primordial soup, when they talk about the origin of life. Does it mean; having accepted the possibility of existence from beginning (primordial) they also (subconsciously) admit the possibility of God's existence, uncreated? I thought one day science as a whole and astronomy in particular, will enable man to understand creation and even the most stubborn and egotistical atheists, would have plenty of unquestionable scientific evidence to accept the existence of God, if scientific evidence is the only way they can see the reality.

*

However, after revising my thoughts regarding the birth of universe, I turned my attention to other question (origin of life) but in doing so I did not find any significant change in the theory or my opinion. I simply could not accept that the accidental merger of a few elements in water or primordial soup could have created the first living creature, (even if it is meant a primitive form of DNA in single cell to begin with). I was delighted to read somewhere that, "Most of the biologists and chemists nowadays are quite confident that the beginning of life on earth was no accident, no rare fluke." The reality is that whether life began on Planet Earth or came from another planet in our galaxy; makes no difference as far as the mystery of creation is concerned. The possibility of DNA coming from another planet or galaxy was hard to believe but I was taught that molecule of DNA could in suitable conditions remain unspoiled for almost one million years. Whether there were such conditions in the hot meteorites no one knows but again, it does not change the essence of question. I had no problem in appreciating and admitting the process explained in Darwinism, even though admittedly there are a few question marks (unless as I will explain later, one looks at it in the context of theism and overall plan of God). However, I still could not perceive how random mutations, could be behind the highly fine-tuned, refined and complex structure of the living things. So, I had (still have) remained with same opinion as before. Recent outstanding discoveries and indeed fascinating findings regarding supernovae have not changed it nor, have they solved the problems of theories. The scientists tell us that; stars die regularly and the new ones are born. When a huge star explodes; from its ashes new stars and their planets are born. The ensuing subatomic particles from supernovae reach our planet and one could say that, in a way, we are all made from stardust. The astronomers say, "The rain of high-speed subatomic and invisible particles and the flood of vast amount of cosmic radiation from supernovae that earth constantly receives, are mutating agents that have shaped the life on earth." It is indeed captivating and breath-taking theory but in my view the effect of no random mutation or accidental factor on genes; could have possibly shaped the life on Planet Earth so precisely. I believe neither above mentioned factors nor stardust and cosmic radiation; could have shaped the life so clearly refined with obvious design in living creatures. In my humble view, the flood of cosmic rays and invisible sub atomic particles that we are regularly bombarded with, could easily explain congenital abnormalities and, genetically acquired diseases in plants, animals and humans as isolated cases but, they could not be the causes of normalities and sophistications, in the structures of living creatures and certainly could not explain the way that life has evolved and shaped on earth.

The more intellectuals talked about their new scientific findings and information, the more I was convinced that life could not be the product of accidents and chance. Regrettably, we have only gathered a small sample of the information hidden in nature and have discovered merely a fraction of the realities in universe but have become arrogantly proud of our knowledge and for what we can see and understand. We mistakenly think that we know a great deal but the truth is quite different. Considering the vast amount yet to be discovered, observed and understood and considering the magnitude of all the information in nature that we have yet to gather and above all considering an ocean of the mysteries, which human longs to resolve; we actually know very little indeed. We are only in the primary stages of a long journey to attain "real knowledge" but we will certainly get there because we have a strong drive for that goal as is illustrated in this quotation, "Man burns to find the secrets of the universe."

However there is no doubt that I am neither in a position nor I would dare to reject the theories of Big Bang and Evolution but whether it was energy first or matter; I strongly believed (and still do) that the former theory was beginning of God's creation and the latter one is within his universal plan and purpose for the creation. In other words, after the birth of single cell creature; the natural and universal evolution was part of God's plan and he guides it. I remained on the same belief as before that; the universal creation and evolution continues but, alongside it (as I will explain later) personal evolution has been left to us within which our mission and destiny reside. Unless some time in future science provides satisfactory answers to the mysteries (that is a possibility I guess) or man evolves, develops and attains the real knowledge through his Divine self; any view about the events before and after Big Bang and emergence of life would be conjectures and imaginations. Having said this, I trust the power of the human brain and believe that, some of man's imaginations could turn out to be exactly what happened and how it all started. I too, like everyone else have imaginations and now adding the latest scientific findings; I wish to present an overall picture of it. This will be in a separate chapter later in the book hoping very much that, the readers would also seriously try to imagine with me even though I ought to admit that, the way I will describe, it may sound too theatrical and simplistic. But let us to continue with revisions, first.

Chapter 9

Revising the questions

Having witnessed, heard and read about the poverty, inequalities, injustices, oppressions, crimes, numerous cruelties and atrocities in human societies throughout the world; I had questioned why God neither prevented them in the past nor does so now. Why did he not create all people to be good right from the beginning? Why does he allow people to do wrong in the first place, if it is true that all our deeds are done with his will and permission? Why did he not create a faultless world in the first place? I had criticised God's inaction in relation to atrocities and criminalities and his apathy and insensitivity, towards assisting the victims of cruelties. I had even dared to accuse him for supporting and siding with autocrats, oppressors and criminals that together with various other factors had led to my retaliating verdict of his nonexistence.   Interestingly, by doing so I had practically withdrawn my objection and questions as it had become inappropriate if there were no God to address questions to.

In revising my thoughts and approach towards these matters, leaving my emotion aside, I found that the questions were at least childish, if not embarrassingly illogical and foolish.   I clearly saw that, my expectations of God and criticisms of his creation were unrealistic and irrelevant, if not shamefully blasphemous. Then I learned that we recognise, comprehend and see the things around us by comparing them with their polar opposites and also because of their relative differences. There is no other way I thought.   Indeed everything in nature could only be seen and identified because of their exact opposites. Good and bad, white and black, lightness and darkness, beauty and ugliness, love and hatred, happiness and sadness had to exist side by side in order to be distinguished and identified.   If from start of human life, contrasts and opposites did not coexist; we could have no idea about anything at all, in the way that we do now. To assess the accuracy and validity of this opinion and scrutinising the point further, I imagined that if everything in the nature were perfect white with no opposite colour of black or any other colour for that matter, and no change in degree of their whiteness; we would not have seen nor distinguished anything at all let alone to have any notion of colour. We could not even have an understanding of white colour nor would we have a name for it. If from the beginning of creation the entire universe was constantly light with no change in intensity and degree of lightness; not only we could not have known what darkness means we couldn't have any understanding of the light either, nor we would be able to see the sun, moon and stars in the heavens and what a great pity that would be! If we, and everything around us had constantly and precisely the same temperature we would not have any idea of the warmth and cold. One could go on with other endless examples of course, but the point is that we can only comprehend and perceive the objects surrounding us; by their polar opposites, proportionalities, their relative differences and contrasts amongst them. There had to be bad, dark and ugly to appreciate good, light and beauty. This is also true for our emotions and feelings, as we could not have known happiness without sorrow, love without hate and there are numerous other examples. Indeed, if we were all created already having the highest possible virtues, having reached the final stage of spiritual and personal development, were already armed with a real knowledge of God and his universal plan and we were all living in spotless and just societies; the creation of human beings would be pointless. Because in that case, we would all be God like and this was not an option in his creation. In such a scenario we could not have had any idea about virtue and vice either, let alone having and using our free will to choose between them and the whole purpose of creation of mankind would have been totally lost. God created human beings with the capability and opportunity to distinguish bad and good, right and wrong, and honoured him by donating the free will, to choose one or the other.   We are responsible and accountable for our deeds and should not blame anyone else (certainly not God) for our wrong doings. In fact the secret of (as well as the instrument for) self-development, evolution, achieving a higher spiritual level and becoming a good human, is this free will and whether or not we would be able to use the freedom of choice correctly in all our deeds and thoughts. Free will is the most important aspect of God's plan as far as the humankind is concerned.   It is only by correct choice between good and bad, between light and darkness, between right and wrong and between the virtues and vices that one could obtain the basic but essential necessities for being a real human.   It is only by distancing from our animal nature and desire, by freeing and empowering our Divine selves that, we could initiate this difficult and long journey of self-development, spiritual elevations and perfection in order to accomplish the mission which we have on this planet. I will return to this point later.

However, I recognized that without coexistence of the right and wrong, good and bad, virtue and vice, beauty and ugliness and above all, without coexistence of love and hatred the odyssey of evolution would have been entirely meaningless and expected achievements irrelevant. So, in revisiting my questions and criticisms of the old days I appreciated that all of injustices, oppressions, cruelties and crimes against the fellow human beings and against other living things, are exclusively consequences of wrong and evil choices made by the perpetrators. Therefore, their wicked thoughts and deeds have got nothing to do with God; except for his prior knowledge of what their actions will be and that is a different matter. I came to this conclusion that, our thoughts and deeds and the choices we make with free will are not predetermined by God and are not written on our foreheads before we are born (despite what I had always been told).   Our actions are not forced upon us by God; we are free men and women hence responsible for our actions and thoughts.   God does not tell or force us to do wrong, nor does he prevent us from doing it.   If wickedness is the choice of some of us but not others, it is simply because; coexistence of the good and bad people is also part of God's overall plan.   We have the freedom of choice for our own actions and hopefully we would make the right ones.   But at the same time it is our duty to establish appropriate educational systems that could teach and encourage us to make the correct choices.   Of course, knowing the shortfalls and failures of the educational systems and limitations in learnings and applying it to our deeds, we must also have the law and order in societies.   This is necessary in order to prevent mischief and punish those who do wrong, commit crimes or cause harm and misery to others, which is exactly what we have already done in most communities.   If these do not work, we should improve the systems not blame God as I had foolishly done.

It is indeed the responsibility of religious and secular leaders of communities to be perfect examples of morality and righteousness, rather than themselves being the offenders of vices and atrocities against the humanity. But it is a great shame to see that over time the majority of leaders and those in power have been examples of latter group of people rather than the former. History shows that their atrocities and crimes have caused far more deaths, destruction and misery in the world than anything else or by any ordinary individual.

Nevertheless, it was clear that most of the questions and objections that I had for God originated from my emotional reaction to social injustices and cruelties that I had witnessed during our political activities. The other reason for that kind of questions was a lack of appreciation of the responsibilities that we all have in establishing just communities. If we have sadly failed in our responsibilities and have allowed the cruel behaviours, wicked deeds and crimes to dominate our societies, it is only our own fault not God's. We deserve the type of educational systems that we establish in our societies or the sort of governments that we elect and allow to rule upon us. God does not choose our ruling systems for us nor does he elect the rulers; we do. God does not side with wicked criminals and tyrants; we (the victims of crimes) allow the perpetrators to commit such atrocities and get away with it. God has not sent different prophets with different messages nor have the prophets brought different religions; we have corrupted, changed and wrongly interpreted and made them so different.   The intellectuals' objection and my reservations in this respect were clearly not justified.

*

In one of the occasional meetings we managed to have, I returned to our conclusions in the last meeting with intellectuals.   They had said because man is weak and afraid of being alone he created God in his mind for the protection and support. In final analysis (as I will address later), I could not accept such simplicity in relation to evolution of the idea of God and his existence in human's mind although I admit our weakness; not because of the fear but for entirely different reasons. That is to say; whenever there is a fault and misery in our lives, we attribute it to God and his failure to prevent such mischief and sorrow. But when all is well and there is joy and satisfaction we forget all about him. If we succeed in a certain task or secure a good position within society or earn wealth and prosperity; not only we do not remember him but we arrogantly congratulate ourselves and attribute attainments to our own intelligence, efforts, skills and cleverness which we just happened to possess. But if we have failure and misfortune, not only we remember God but we also either blame him for our misery or more likely beg for his assistance. Interestingly, in such circumstances even the atheists seek his help and expect miracles. In that sense I would entirely agree with the intellectuals that we are weak creatures. But the weakness is not the real reason behind the emergence of idea of God in human's mind, (more about that later).

I had questioned whether God could be seen. In returning to this question and revisiting my thoughts, I arrived at exactly the same conclusion as before. I believed then, and still do that God, as Jesus said, could not be seen and the teachings of Islam confirm this. Ironically, I also believed and continue to believe that God could be seen but not by physical eyes. The inner self and intuitive mind could see him; if one rises to the higher levels. Even without significant spiritual achievements, we all have an image of God in our minds. However, the main reason why most of us cannot see God is that, at the level we are; it is impossible to stand the ecstasy derived from seeing the absolute beauty and endure the intensity of such an experience. Whenever I read or hear about those people who claim that they had vision of 'God' my usual attitude and reaction towards them is sceptical and distrustful. I seriously believe that majority if not all of these claimed visions of God are false and merely for the purpose of self-aggrandizement. The best I could do for them is to say that, such visions are either dreams and illusions or a product of alcohol and drugs. I admit that with this harsh attitude towards other people's reported visions, I should not mention anything in that category, which could have slightest resemblance to such claims. But, I am afraid I have to refer to one of my dreams and very much hope that, readers would kindly appreciate that it is necessary for the point I am about to make. This is in fact the second dream that is mentioned in this book and I do hope it will not be required to refer to any more. It is a very short dream and I emphasise, it is only a dream and I bring here only to explain a very important point.

I was passing through a darkish and narrow lane or, perhaps a bazaar when in turning the corner suddenly a dazzling light hit my eyes. It seemed that the rays of light were coming from a small crack on the wall. The scene in this dream was very simple to observe and yet without slightest exaggeration it was the most beautiful and most perfect thing that I had ever witnessed. The feeling was virtually the same as I had in the other dream which was mentioned before but this time with far more intensity. The light although was dazzling but at the same time it was the most comforting, tranquillising and most pleasantly warm thing that, produced a powerful and indescribable happiness in me and instantly filled my whole being. Every single cell of my body was saturated with the bliss. I had a vivid idea and understanding that it was God's light. The intensity of ecstasy which I was experiencing was indeed intolerable and I honestly felt and feared that, my heart was bursting off my chest from the gravity of such an extreme experience. I had a strange feeling that every single cell of my body was swollen and saturated with the bliss and due to intensity of indescribable felicity I really thought that I was just about to be totally annihilated, when I suddenly woke up. It took some time before my body returned to normal state. I'm sure the defensive mechanism that we all have and continue to work while we are sleep, woke me up to save my life. The entire dream lasted only for a couple of seconds and the time that I was actually exposed to that ineffable beauty and ecstasy, was just a fraction of a second and yet, I have no doubt that if I had not woken up I would have died. Years later as I write these words, indeed in the very moment; I have a vivid memory of that utmost pleasant experience, of that inspiring and unique joy and its intolerable intensity. The point I would like to make will follow after the next few sentences. Although in that dream, it was very difficult to look at the light but even seeing it for merely a fraction of a second revealed such an ineffable beauty and caused such an effect on me that it is impossible to put into the words. Believe me that beauty continues to affect my mind even today, and the intensity of bliss that I experienced is indescribable. The pleasant feeling of that heavenly experience is certainly incomparable with any type of pleasure and happiness that, I have ever had in my life and without any exaggeration, miles above the climax of most extreme pleasure in earthly life that one could think of. And yet it was only a short dream, it was only my assumption that the light was radiating from 'God' and the whole experience of being exposed to such happiness was only for a fraction of a second. What would have been the effect; if it were in real life and not a dream, if it were for a longer period of time and not for a fraction of a second? If this experience was just a glimpse of the true happiness that one would have in seeing of perfect beauty of God then it clearly explains why we cannot see him. It is simply because; at the lower levels of our development and evolution we couldn't endure the effects of such an experience. But if we ever achieved perfection then, we would be able to behold that perfect beauty and tolerate the intensity of ultimate ecstasy. I came to believe that, the personal evolution and spiritual elevation, leading to the perfect human,

211

is attainable but it is not so easy for the reasons that I will discuss later on.   In that stage of the journey, when I was revising my thoughts, questions and the objections to God, I also revised other matters such as the Judgement day, Heaven, Hell, logic of worship and praying.   But at this point of narration I would like to continue with the idea of God.

Chapter 10

The idea of God

The idea of God with all its seriousness and complexity (as the most fundamental matter for humankind) had been simplified by the intellectuals and, merely attributed to man's fear, especially when left alone, his need for a supernatural power to protect him and his natural inclination, to adore and worship something or someone.

More seriously though, some thinkers had researched, scrutinised and analysed the origin of the idea of God and its evolution within the human's mind. They had traced it back to, first (the fear), then to (the respect) and finally (the worship) of ancestors, dead parents, dead chieftains of tribes or villages and dead kings. The researchers had suggested that, after a long period of time, the focus of worship changed to the ghosts and relics of such important personalities. Later on, the stones

213

that were laid on their graves were worshipped, steadily moving to sticks laid upon the graves and the trees that grew beside them and so on and so forth.   I have no intention to dispute such views and indeed, I see no point in conflicting with whatever they suggest about the result of research nor the way that they suggest how the idea of God evolved over the time.   But I cannot accept their conclusion, regarding the existence or nonexistence of God, which I find totally irrelevant and inappropriate to the nature of their own findings. As the researchers and thinkers argue, it is quite possible **that,** everything started from the fear of the dead body (hence, the idea of burying corpse and putting heavy stone on the graves to prevent the harm that might arise from the returning of the dead person) **that,** decades or centuries later changed to a respect for the corpses of their parents, leaders, chieftains or kings. I could also accept **that ,** as time passed such respects changed to worship of their ghosts and relics (the skull in particular) and stone laid on their graves (hence, the origin of sacred stones and stone gods) and trees grown beside the graves (hence, the origin of sacred trees) as their gods. For the sake of important points which I would like to raise shortly, I don't even mind accepting their suggestion **that,** perhaps all of such objects of worship, many handmade idols or manufactured gods and sacred animals or natural powers that were worshipped steadily, merged to a single deity like Yahweh residing inside the Ark (hence, beginning of the monotheism) **that,** finally led to the merger of Jesus to the God of Hebrews. Anyone of these suggestions and results of further researches to explain origin of the idea of God in human's mind and why he manufactured gods and finally how the idea of God evolved over the long time, would make no difference to this view, which I put to the intellectual of café Naderi.

"One could actually afford to accept all of your suggestions as the likelihood of emerging this idea of God in human's mind. But in my opinion, the major error of the researchers is the way that they reach to their conclusions. That is to say; using the findings of their research as solid base for rejecting God and suggesting that man made it up. If human beings couldn't understand the true nature of this idea that had entered into his rational or intuitive mind and therefore, assumed that whoever or whatever frightened and impressed them was God; merely shows his failure to understand. If man thought whoever seemed more powerful and ruled over him or simply seemed mysterious ought to be worshipped or should be pleased and bribed by offering of gifts and sacrifices, does not mean that there is no God. It only means that human bitterly failed to see the Truth and grasp the idea of God in his mind; a failure that continues to be the case even today. Truly if such a lack of comprehension led to the manufacturing of gods and goddesses in bizarre shapes and to worshipping of their own hand-made gods with appalling rituals and sacrifices; how on earth could one conclude that God does not exist? Logically it merely confirms the inability of humans to comprehend such an idea. If man adapted the extraordinary sacramental practices with unbelievable barbarity (in order to please his gods and goddesses), this would add to our shames as humans but, by no means has it got anything to do with the question of God's existence.   It is absolutely clear to me that whatever primitive people thought about the nature of God; is totally irrelevant to our principal question.   Indeed, whoever they chose or manufactured as god and however they worshiped; makes no difference either.   All they do confirm is humanity's failure to correctly analysis that idea and find logical answers to his questions and I'm afraid that religions did not solve his problem either". The patience of the dismayed intellectuals to hear my arguments in silence was remarkable, they hardly uttered a word!

*

I genuinely believe that, the idea of God came to the rational mind of primitive humans through their intuitive minds and inner selves for entirely different reasons and not because of fear. But not knowing what it was man acted in a manner that today, appears to us ridiculous, illogical and unacceptable. In revising this issue and debating with the intellectuals, I realized that the atheists used every possible argument to deny God, yet not a single one was directly related to the question of God's existence. If they referred to the admittedly ridiculous topics and nonsense in some of the sacred books or, if they tried to prove the absurdity and falsehood of religions and denied the prophecy of the prophets, or, if they analysed the origin of the idea of God in human's mind and the way such an idea evolved; I could not see how they could relate all these to the nonexistence of God. Therefore, I said to intellectuals that none of their arguments and explanations could validate their claims or provide any justification for the denial of God. The atheists were not amused at all with such a declaration, nor were they pleased to hear my boldly expressed opinion. "I believe; every single human in the entire history, has thought

218

about God regardless of belief or disbelief in his existence and this is absolutely unrelated to fears or respect to any person or any object. God came to the rational mind of human, because of the presence of inner self and intuitive mind. I believe that when in the process of universal evolution humans emerged on earth, God had already bestowed to them a part of his own being, in order to establish their real selves (Divine selves), which I think is the same as soul. This is the part of humans that possesses the intuitive mind and in my belief it is the direct route of communications and relationship with God. And that, quite naturally, is exactly the reason why the idea of God entered into man's mind. In other words such an idea came into the mind because a tiny portion of God's spirit already existed in him. But man, with the rational mind of his physical self, could neither appreciate nor comprehend what that idea was. Hence all the misinterpretations, the manufacturing of false gods, the adoption of appalling and disgraceful rituals, and worse still; the barbaric practices of

219

presenting human sacrifices to their man-made gods, which would be equally wrong were it for the real God".

The intellectuals had repeatedly referred to the naivety and barbarity of primitive people and, their superstitious belief or practiced rituals, in order to ridicule and insult theists and all religious people, whatever their religion. So, I had to repeat that failure of primitive people and our own failure even today, to understand the true God, and therefore, inventing false ones and adopting strange ways of worship should not be taken as valid reasons to prove the accuracy of their views.

*

It was around this time of journey that, I had exhausted reviewing different schools of thought and views. But in debates with my friends I had not referred to them, as I wished to express my own opinion without quoting from philosophers or scholars. The majority of these schools of thought and arguments whether scientific, philosophical, cosmological, ontological, theological or teleological, are definitely relevant in debates and indeed all of them by different routes confirm that God exists. However, with due respect to philosophers and scientists behind these schools of thought, I found the evidence of my inner self, intuitive mind and conscience far more convincing. There is a sentence in the book of (Transforming light by A .Vail and E. Vail) that refers to the same point; "God is not a hypothesis but a reality that he may be known in the same direct way in which one recognizes the true love as a feeling in mind". That is true; God is not a hypothesis to be proved scientifically; He is a reality. Amongst all these arguments I was more interested in the teleological argument, which refers to the purpose, design and order in universe and inevitably to the existence of designer. Scientific evidence to support this opinion is abundant of course, but again, for me nothing was as convincing and as clear as the evidence of the Cup of Jam. Having said so, for the first time in our debates and only to encourage them to come out of their ivory towers if at all possible; I talked about the teleological argument. Having combined the principals of that argument with my belief regarding the role of inner self in generating the idea of God in human's mind, I referred to a quotation, which is said Cicero gave from Aristotle. Whether he was mistaken in attributing it to Aristotle or not the example is excellent one in this respect. The quotation is about a people that hypothetically lived for ages in the dark underground, where they heard of some unknown supernatural being called god. With this idea in mind they came out of the darkness and faced with the light and magnificent nature and predictably credited all these wonders and beauties to same idea of god in their mind. Here, I said to my infidel friends, Cicero implies that; the idea of God is not derived from our observations of the order in universe or, because of the beauties and wonders in nature but rather, it is confirmed and substantiated by such observations. Then I referred to this statement in teleological arguments.

222

"Intellect, conscience and the experience of beauty suggest the teleological order of universe and the directive mind which is God." Finally I quoted a sentence from Thomas Aquinas. "There is an intellectual being by which all natural things, even though they do not have power of knowing themselves, are directed towards that end. And this we call God." Then, I asked them, is it not true to say that, today scientists have proved the reality of design in universe? And if that is the case, is it not also true that there should be a designer too? The philosophers of course, have referred to God by different terms and names such as; The First Cause, The Whole, The Infinite Being, Perfect Being or Directive Mind, The Necessary Being and The Most Real Being. But, in my dialogue with the intellectuals, I settled with the word God to avoid the confusion that in my youth arose. I must admit that, they were not impressed by my quotations but, I thought they were pleased when they heard me murmuring; "The point at which, we become sure that, God exists in our thoughts as well as our practical life, is precisely the moment when we cannot do without him." Those intellectuals, having expressed their disappointment of my regression once again tried to enlighten me and save my status in society. Therefore, to engage me in further debates they asked this question. "Why the humans can't understand God as you imply, and if he really exists, why does he not present himself somehow so that, even we could tolerate his majestic image and believe in him?" The latter part of their question was of course, sarcastic. I answered them with my belief, without being too concerned about their reactions and whether or not they would be pleased to hear it or take any notice of my views, which in fact they did not. Thereafter, I no longer received the same welcome, nor respect from them in their meetings. What did I say that made them wish to throw me out of their circle? Well, I told them what seemed to me to be a fact; the fact that remains my belief even today. "There are reasons why man is not able to understand God, define his nature, visualise his image or see him." Then,

I continued to reply to the dismay of intellectuals and expressed my opinion in some detail.   "I believe man is an extremely small portion of God and "the portion" or "part" cannot have any understanding or conception of "the whole". I asked them to imagine an electron "the portion" inside a huge and highly complex machine "the whole" where; this electron is circulating around the nucleus of an atom that itself is part of a molecule.   Knowing that such a tiny thing together with several trillions of other electrons, atoms and molecules, make up the machine "whole" I asked them as I had asked myself many times; how could this electron (if for the sake of argument had brain and intelligence) have any idea about the shape, colour, weight, size and function of the machine? The electron (portion in this scenario) could certainly find out about itself and other electrons.   It could even find out about the protons and neutrons inside the atom around which our electron is circulating and at the most it could perhaps, have some idea about similar or different atoms inside the molecule that this electron belongs to. But I can see no way that our poor electron "portion" could imagine or find out the exact nature, shape, dimensions and function of the machine "whole". Unless of course, (again theoretically and for the sake of debate) it could develop to, much higher levels; attain special power and skills, break the walls that surround it, come out of its prison and observe the machine from outside. Our imaginary electron "portion" neither would have any idea about the machine "whole" nor would have any aspiration and willingness to discover the whole's structure and secrets, unless of course, it regards attaining the real knowledge (in this example knowledge about machine) as a mission for itself. It is only then that this electron (or human if we now leave the poor electron alone and talk about man) having realized that he has a mission to fulfil and, having realized that self-development and evolution are vehicles for the fulfilment of such a mission; he will certainly embark on the journey in order to understand the "whole" that is God. As for the sarcastic part of their question "Why does God not show himself?" I reminded them of my dream and the point that I had made there, concluding that; no undeveloped man could tolerate the intensity of such an experience; unless, he begins to evolve and elevate to much higher levels which is indeed the essence of man's mission.

Understandably after this meeting I couldn't meet these committed atheist intellectuals as often as I used to, because I was not one of them anymore. As I said earlier, they didn't completely throw me out of their society because our political links were strong. Therefore, I will still refer to their thoughts and comments in the following chapters when I find appropriate; quoting from the discussions which we had for many years and also from the occasional meetings and debates that, I was able to arrange following the last (from their point of view disastrous debate) that we had about the idea of God. Having said so, shortly afterwards the political circumstances changed a great deal and as will come later in the narration and

regular meetings were resumed for totally different reasons.

Chapter 11

Imaginations

Throughout this journey, based on partial information and knowledge, I often tried to imagine how the whole thing began and even dared to hypothesise the design, purpose and conditions surrounding God's creation. I tried to find out; what is the mankind's mission on earth and what is our destiny. Sometimes, I put these to the intellectuals of Café Naderi to see what their reactions and views were. But whatever I said and thought about the nature of God, how and why he created the universe in the first place and why human beings are on this planet, they rejected them all as speculation, conjecture and surely non-scientific arguments and very rightly so. I say very rightly so, because for most of us it is almost impossible to answer these questions accurately. Indeed for the majority of people God is incomprehensible, inconceivable, indefinable and indescribable. Moreover, his universal design and purpose of creation are unattainable secrets that; make understanding of man's mission and significance of fulfilling it so difficult to grasp.   Doubts and uncertainties about the accuracy of our understanding of these matters and doubts about validity of the interpretation and answers to fundamental questions will always remain with us. Unless one attains perfection but that is a different matter for later in the book.   Having said so, doubts in our minds and the difficulties of providing fitting answers to these mysteries and even the dominance of animal selves in our lives, have never been serious obstacles for the man in his constant effort to find the Truth, nor have they prevented his imagination or rationalisation in order to come up with theories, ideas and beliefs.   In spite of the fact that it is impossible to know precisely; how the universe and life came to existence, almost everyone has thought about these burning questions and has shaped a sort of picture in his mind.   Before narration of the far more serious part of this journey, at this point, I would like to reveal my personal version of imagination. I must mention some of the matters which follow have been stated earlier and some will be revealed in the next chapters. Therefore, I will only refer to those points in passing. In order to imagine and dare to hypothesise as to how it all began, I reflected on the information I had attained from books, scientists, mystics, philosophers, astronomers, theologians and several other sources. I hoped that in so doing my imagination would be as close as possible to the Truth. From what I have said in previous chapters, readers would appreciate that in my vision, the Divine self and intuitive mind are bound to play their central roles. As I requested earlier, I do hope that from here on, the readers will patiently join me in imagining.

To begin with I remembered the stories my mother told me as a child and every single one of them began with a sentence in Azeri language that has almost the same meaning as, "Once upon a time, there was no one but the God." I have no doubt, that in every other language, there is a similar sentence with which mothers begin their stories. I thought that is precisely where I should start my imaginings. But there was another factor that played a role in initial scene of my imagination and that was the word used for God in the Persian language, which is Khoda. (Khod) means self and (a) refers to the coming and therefore, (Khoda) means the one who came to existence on his own. It seemed to me very interesting that hundreds or thousands years ago when the founders of this language were thinking of an appropriate word to assign to God, they came up with a term that clearly implies God is an uncreated entity and reality. Therefore, my imaginings begin with these two points in mind. That is to say; before the beginning of time nothing existed except for God and he was not created.

About twelve or thirteen billion years ago there was nothing in the universe and cosmos, as known to us today.

There was complete emptiness, vacuum and nothingness. Virtually nothing existed, nothing what so ever except for God. And God was absolute beauty; truly the essence of beauty, glory and majesty. He was the source of wisdom, intelligence, power, energy and creativity. Within God's creativity and power, potentially there were innumerable beautiful things to build and display, precious words to say, sacred secrets to disclose and more than anything else there was potentially an overwhelming happiness to present to the entities other than himself in order that they could enjoy the experience. But how the nothingness and emptiness could be addressed by those precious words? And how could the nothingness be intimate to those sacred secrets? How could the emptiness receive and appreciate those beautiful things and treasures, and how could the nothingness experience the happiness? God had the most attractive and beautiful light but how could the vacuum, reflect it? God was the source and essence of existence and he was most compassionate and generous. He was all of these

233

attributes, qualities and many more which are beyond my ability to express and complete such a long list, even in my imagination.   How could the nothingness and vacuum appreciate those attributes?

*

The nature and image of God cannot be accurately described because, he is not like any shape or form that we know and recognise in this world, even though, we all have vague image of him in our inner selves. We recognise and differentiate the things because of their polar opposites and so; based on this concept one can argue that because God is (the whole) and has no (polar opposite) therefore we cannot know him. But no, in my imagination and analysis we cannot know God nor have clear image of him because (the portion) that we are cannot have an accurate understanding of (the whole) that, he is. Having said so, if I wanted to use the notion of polar opposite to explain the same point, I could have said; in fact,

God has polar opposites that are nothingness and non-existence but, because we have no shape or image of nothingness and non-existence in our minds we cannot have a shape or form of their opposites either and that means we cannot have true recognition of God and an accurate image of him. In my imagination, I preferred the former. To explain how God came to existence without a creator, some may say that, because everything must have its opposite; nothingness and vacuum had to bring out their opposites to existence too and that was the wholeness, God. But these are not the explanations that I would consider even in my imaginings. However, there was God and he was alone in the absolute emptiness, vacuum and nothingness. He was the creator, but without any creature; to whom could he be God? Moreover, without creation would there be any meaning, value or use of having the ultimate power and creativity? In other words, in my mind the act of creation was the logical and inevitable consequence of his being and existence; in fact, it was the only option in that

235

sense. But I also thought that there was another reason for creation. And that was the absolute beauty of God which could potentially generate pure love and infinite happiness. And God with his utmost generosity, unselfishness and compassion wished to make that happiness; a real possibility. But again, without the existence of a being other than God himself, to observe, appreciate and love such a perfect beauty and experience that ultimate and endless happiness there could be no use for quality of perfect beauty in God's being either. As he was above any kind of need and, self- indulgence had no place in his being therefore, God planned to make others happy. And such "others" were still non-existent in absolute emptiness of today's cosmos and therefore, had to be created first; to present the happiness to those creatures. There had to be creatures capable of appreciating God's gift. The fact is that, if there were no perfect beauty, absolute love and possibility of ultimate bliss, there would be no creation either. God had all the ingredients to bring infinite ecstasy to those "others" and so, he began his creation of the universe in total nothingness. It was a grand design and he knew who would evolve in the universe, to receive the everlasting happiness.

God wished to create matter first and there it was (instantly); enough matter to create all the galaxies. He condensed the matter in a small ball to begin with.   Some people might say that he first created the energy that following gigantic explosion converted to matter. But in my imagination matter was created first, simply because the energy was already in God's own being and did not need to be created.   Of course, this does not reject their opinion because one could argue that, God used some of his own energy for such an explosion and conversion to matter.   However, in my imagination having first created matter he put some of his own energy into the ball of condensed matter which immediately, caused the huge explosion that today we call the Big Bang. And this was the beginning of "time" as we understand now (do we? I wonder). This explosion produced extremely large clouds of mist and tiny particles of the dust that, instantly spread in the emptiness and moved away from the centre of explosion with an incredible speed; creating vast space and billions of galaxies with trillions of suns and planets in each one of them; all according to God's wonderful design. The explosion was so massive that, even today, the astronomers can detect and record cosmic background radiations and other evidence related to such a gigantic surge. A gigantic explosion by which; the birth of an amazing universe was announced in total emptiness and nothingness. Astronomers believe that galaxies continue to move away from the centre, because of the force generated by the Big Bang but they also say that, eventually the space will shrink and all galaxies will return to their origin that is condensed matter in a small ball. Some say this shrinking or collapsing has already begun. This is an amazing theory and I may return to this point later, but the reality is that everything that astronomers see in the universe is not as it is now but as it was in the past. Indeed every telescope is a time machine, and one cannot easily determine, whether space and universe within the cosmos is expanding at the present time or shrinking to collapse. I personally imagine that galaxies have already stopped moving away from the centre of explosion and the evidence that, we record today is what was happening billions years ago. In fact I believe that, they are now arranged in a meticulous order, precisely where God intended them to be. I must admit that it is impossible to even imagine why it was necessary to create billions of galaxies and within them, trillions of suns and planets, unless of course, we stop assuming that earth is centre of the universe and by so doing, begin to consider other possibilities.

I don't have clear imagining about other galaxies but in the galaxy, in which Planet Earth resides, five billion years ago the Sun was born from clouds of gas and dust and almost at the same time, its family of planets came to the being that included

Earth. According to the universal plan of God, Earth settled an ideal distance from sun as it was here that life destined to begin and evolve. It was here that the final product of evolution was planned to live; an evolved creature who would be the receiver of God's gifts. Therefore about 3.8 billion years ago the first living thing appeared on Planet Earth, in the form of a single cell with a preliminary form of DNA molecule in it; capable of reproduction. And then the universal evolution began as God had planned. It is very likely that life in some form or other was created in other galaxies too or even in other planets of our own galaxy but one could not be certain without having attained the real knowledge of God or perhaps, science will find an answer to that question in future. But according to my imagination there is no reason why Earth should be the only planet in the entire universe to have such a privilege. I often remembered the idea of DNA coming from another planet and imagined may be God created much higher level of life and intelligence elsewhere in this universe that were or are so advanced in science and technology that they could transfer their DNA to Earth without damaging it. Then I said to myself no; man and his brain is God's masterpiece and if there were life elsewhere in universe; they ought to be inferior to us. This is I admit an egotistic assumption. Following the Big Bang and the formation of galaxies, suns, planets and their moons it took about 8 billion years before the life was born on Earth and it took more than 3.5 billion years before human beings emerged through evolution. It may seem a long period of time but for God it is a very short time, if time is relevant in his case in the first place. For us, time begins with the Big Bang but the reality is that time is the by-product of human's mind and I confess that it is too difficult for me to correctly comprehend it.

When the human emerged from the evolution, God loved him. They say God created man in his own image and this might be the reason why he loved him but I find that difficult to accept. I don't think that God, in the process of evolution, made the human to look like his own image nor that was the reason why he loved him. Such notion that God loved man because he resembled him; implies that he is selfish and arrogant, which is not the case. The root of such suggestion could be found in egocentrism of man. But of course, my belief that human and his brain are masterpiece of God's creation could also be attributed to same attitude. However based on that notion, it is obvious why God loved human. We all love our masterpieces, don't we? All artists (those who create music and painting or anything else for that matter) love their own works. And if they do not love all of them, there is no doubt that they love their masterpiece. So God loved man and granted him an incredibly advanced brain, wisdom, conscience, soul and intuitive mind. The soul of man that was from the wholeness of God's own soul; established his Devine self and "she" chose the molecule of DNA, that by this time had become amazingly a complex and sophisticated structure, for

242

her dwelling place. She also used this molecule as a vehicle to pass this highly precious donation of God to the subsequent generations of humankind.   God presented all polar opposites to human in his earthly life and gave him free will, to choose between the good and bad. Intentionally man was created to be an imperfect creature and some part of the animal nature from earlier stages of evolution had to remain in his being.   But he had also the potential to evolve further and become pure and perfect.   And that was indeed the "mission" that God had assigned to him.   Right from the beginning; soul longed to return to her origin to unite and, became a driving force in development of the humankind towards the perfection and merger with his source, which is God.   When it says in The Quran that, "we are from God and to whom we will return.", surely it means that man (or to be precise, his soul) will return to God.   But if it that sentence meant the entire creation will return to God then, the theory presented by some astronomers would be very stimulating; when they say eventually the universe will shrink and collapse. This is a frightening possibility I thought. Is it likely that after billions of years all the galaxies will return to the centre of initial explosion and once again will become same condensed matter ready to be exploded again? Could this mean that the entire process will be repeated and each time God will cause the "explosion and creation", all over again, and the cycle will go on and on forever? If that is the case; why? However, human beings turned out to be very complicated creatures. He had a highly developed brain that had the potential to be at the service of his false self (a smart servant to the animalistic side of his being). But at the same time he had an intuitive mind, soul and conscience to evolve his humanity and communicate with God. Indeed, man was a strange mixture of perfection and imperfection; ready to go either way.

God reflected his pure light and beauty through nature so that humans could sense his presence everywhere and believe in him.   He also provided all worldly pleasures, love and happiness (but only in short lived and to a lesser degree), so that humans could experience and become aware of them. The co-existence of good and bad together with the free will were essential for the personal development and evolution of man in relation to his mission.   It was in the nature of humans to love beauty and feel   happiness but as such pleasures were in partial forms on Earth man had to develop and evolve first, to be capable of appreciating perfect beauty and tolerating the intensity of real happiness.   It was also man's exceptional quality to discover the information and secrets of nature, and to experience joy and satisfaction of attaining knowledge, even though these would be merely partial too. The happiness derived from attaining the "real knowledge", if man succeeds in his mission and meets his destiny, is beyond my imagination. So, the mission was that the imperfect human, with his free will, would face the choice between wrong and right. Then by choosing the good and right he would develop towards perfection and by attaining the real knowledge, seeing ineffable beauty, feeling true love, and being in the presence of God; he would experience absolute peace and infinite happiness.   Regrettably, although God had generously provided all the necessary assistance to make man's personal development possible; his animal self, proved to be the dominant side of his being and earthly pleasures fascinated him. Indeed he acted more like animals than human. So God inspired philosophers, artists and scientists in order to enable humans to fulfil their mission.   God also inspired and appointed prophets to guide and lead the man in right direction and help him to comprehend his task. Sadly, man found it extremely difficult (and still does) to fully understand why he is on Earth. He found it difficult to appreciate that the earthly pleasures of love and happiness are partial, false and mere shadows in this world. He could not understand they are only provided here to prepare him for real ones. He was not supposed to be attached to false happiness in his earthly life but he did and showed ignorance of his mission.

God's creation continues as does his universal evolution. And I imagine that, in millions or billions of years eventually, there will be a perfect creature that will be able to see all the qualities of God and will attain all the secrets. That creature will experience the perfect happiness that God wished to present to the "others". However, at the same time, God made it potentially possible for human to reach that last stage, ahead of the final outcome of evolution, if he could realize his mission and act upon it. The sad reality is that with the exception of certain prophets, in spite of all his assistance and guidance, only a few people in their quest for perfection have ever reached the summit. This is because, for the imperfect human, attraction of temporary and easily accessible earthly pleasures, were too powerful to ignore, so for him, distancing himself from these partial pleasures seemed almost impossible, without higher motives.   The problem was (and continues to be) that human societies have hardly ever managed to comprehend and embrace higher motives.   Of course, many people have conquered the initial stages of self-development and evolution, and there is a real chance and hope that such a trend would continue and even improve in the near future.

*

In my imagination I could neither see Heaven nor Hell.   I assumed that the prophets had to use ordinary words and popular examples from earthly life to show the excellence of life in paradise by referring to gardens, flowers, fruits, food, wine and beautiful women or handsome men.   I imagined that if a person fulfilled his mission and became at least a real human (if not perfect) he would enjoy living in Heaven - while on earth.   And when he died, his soul in DNA, would continue in that pleasant state until DNA decays, and the soul would return to God in order to live in the infinite felicity.   And Hell,

248

could be regarded as being deprived from all this.   As for the resurrection in judgement day, although God is able to do anything he wanted, (including bringing all the dead to life for trial, punishment or rewards) but in my imagination, I could not see any necessity for such day; as God already knows who should be rewarded and who should be punished.   Now, let us return to narrative and more serious matters. What am I saying? The imagination was about the same serious matters anyway, was it not?   I hope the readers embarked on their own imaginations, while reading this chapter.

Chapter 12

The mission

In previous chapters of this book I've repeatedly referred to man's "mission" on this planet and have more or less explained this. But now it is time to expound on it in some detail. What I mean by mission or perhaps more appropriately what is my understanding of it. One of the fundamental questions that had occupied a significant part of my thoughts and debates with the intellectuals of café Naderi was whether, the emergence of man on Planet Earth was entirely an accidental matter or was it following creator's design and purpose including allocation of a mission for him. The adamant intellectuals strongly believed that the matter was purely an accidental event. They tried to make me comprehend that, over a three-billion-year history of life, evolution led to emergence of humans on this planet and simply by rules of natural selection and random mutations he

251

happened to retain a highly developed brain, intelligence and conscience. They said that there is no creator, no plan, no purpose and definitely no mission and all we ought to do is to enjoy the life as best and as much as we can. They seriously believed that people would be better off if they stopped wasting their time and efforts by having useless arguments about God, religion and faith and get on with their materialistic lives. "We should," said the intellectuals with utmost confidence, "thankfully use humanity's hard earned discoveries and achievements to make life even more meaningful and enjoyable and, forget about all this nonsense that you keep repeating." It was very interesting to hear them saying (to make life meaningful) obviously, they meant this materialistically. They were concerned only with their own hedonistic lives. As for the debates and expression of views they generously granted themselves every right, to talk against the religions and God, to the extent of offending the believers, but would ridicule anyone else outside the circle, if he thought and seriously talked about such matters and any other metaphysical issue. Clearly, I could not agree with them and would not accept that man with such brain, this wonderful machine, emerged on earth only to satisfy the demands of his animal nature. I couldn't accept that there was no design and purpose behind the creation of man and couldn't endorse the atheists' statement that man have no mission in his earthly life except to enjoy materialism.

As I mentioned before I simply could not accept this opinion that natural selection and random mutations could explain an incredible and massive jump in development of the brain (structurally) or mind (functionally) from apes to humans. I kept repeating commonly asked questions. Where did we come from, how did we get here, where are we going and is there any purpose behind our emergence on this planet? My busy intellectual friends had no time for this type of questions and they did not want to fall behind the others in gaining more pleasures in such a competitive materialistic world and I must say that their attitude was no surprise to me. The power and influence of worldly pleasures and happiness (even though partial, superficial and short lived) and the attractiveness of materialistic life and transitory euphoria of human experiences (while attending his animal desires); are so strong, appealing and satisfying that most of people find little appetite, time and indeed necessity for anything else.   Some of the intellectuals in our society, like many others outside it, would not take a break to seriously contemplate about anything different and would hardly bother themselves (long enough) with matters such as the unseen world or metaphysical matters. Such individuals merely believe and accept what they see with their physical eyes and value only the things that, would give them instant profit, pleasure and satisfaction.   Their philosophy is quite simple; only believe in what you see and value what gives you pleasure and profit.   As the mystics say, "Man is so absorbed in what he sees that, he doubts the vast realities that he does not see." This is indeed, a fitting statement that was precisely applicable to some of the intellectuals of Café Naderi. However, the practical problem is that at lower levels of development, at the primary stages of evolution and early steps of our spiritual elevations, we can neither truly understand God nor can we correctly define him. Neither can we fully appreciate the perfect design of universe nor could we wholeheartedly and continuously believe in the existence of a creator behind the beauties, delicacies and precisions in nature. Nor could we understand the logic and the necessity of design and purpose behind such a magnificent creation. So, how could we recognize the mission for human beings and appreciate the significance of its fulfilment? Having said that, if a person (with normal intelligence), sincerely believed that, God exists and has created the entire universe; surely he will also appreciate and admit that, such an outstanding work, (even though we have neither unravelled its secrets nor have fully appreciated its glory and splendours) could not have been without a plan and purpose. Indeed, it is the duty of man to find the answer to this question; "what is the nature of this plan and its purpose?"

*

At the time that I was seriously contemplating these matters; the society of intellectuals of Café Naderi had changed a lot. A few middle-aged men and women had occasional meetings, mostly to talk about politics of the day as one could sense that "revolution" was on its way. Some of our friends had fled the country, some had been executed or died under the tortures, some were still imprisoned and others had given up their political activities and, had chosen self-imposed isolation and house arrest. The remaining members had no appetite for the metaphysical matters and in any case I did not meet them as often. By then of course, I thought that I had passed the first stage, which was certainty about the existence of God and for the next stages, I really did not think they could be of any help.

It was about this phase of the journey that without a shadow of doubt I was convinced that not only God exists but also he has a plan and purpose for his creation. Having arrived to this firm conviction I assumed that I was ready for a deeper search. What could be God's plan and purpose for his creation and what is their relevance and links to human beings? I asked myself.   Atheists may not bother about this part of my narration of course, but as theists, when we remember that God is source, meaning and essence of wisdom, intelligence, power, energy, creativity, light, beauty, kindness, love, mercy and justice; we would appreciate that he could not have created the entire universe for himself, as he is beyond any need, nor would he have done it without any plan and purpose.   Unlike what the atheist intellectuals said and ridiculed, God did not create the universe and human beings in it, as toys for his own amusement nor did he do so merely for the sake of creation to practice his skill.   He created all for a reason and I believe the following picture is a possibility.   I say a possibility and I honestly mean it, as I would not go beyond that at this phase of a long journey as a mere beginner.   Truly, only those who have reached the highest spiritual levels would know the answers to secrets with certainty.   Of course, I am conscious that, this "possible picture" has already been described, in the chapter designated to my imagination but now I don't merely imagine, I believe.   In the preface of book, I mentioned that there will be reiterations of certain points; as not only circumstances and scientific information were changing but the ideas and beliefs were changing, evolving or maturing too.

I believe that; absolute beauty within God's own existence had to be seen and appreciated, that, real love had to be felt and acknowledged, that, infinite felicity had to be experienced and finally a creature capable of developing to receive and enjoy all these gifts had to be created otherwise; what would be the use or meaning of all those qualities in God?   There had to be someone other than God himself for these privileges and happiness as he is beyond self-indulgence. Therefore, God devised a grand plan and created the entire universe and life in it to produce that (creature) through the evolution so that someone other than himself could receive those gifts. Of course, we do not yet know the precise circumstances and Truth about the creation, but surely we could use all available scientific information to rationalise and refer to our inner selves to unravel some of the secrets. Or at least, we could use our imaginations, which is what I often did and a summary of this was described in an earlier chapter. But at this stage of the narrative, I would like to leave that line aside, and take a shortcut into the matters related to man's mission and destiny based on a hypothetical assumption that man is the only candidate to experience true love and infinite ecstasy, as we have no idea whether there are other living creatures elsewhere in the universe. Real happiness, felicity, bliss, joy and ecstasy (or any other word that could do justice to the exact meaning and quality of such an emotional state and define its intensity) could be possible only by facing the absolute beauty and pure light, by experiencing true love and, by acquiring real knowledge of God and the secrets of his creation. But no creature, anything less than God himself, could perceive those qualities without a prior exposure and experience in earthly pleasures and without preparation nor could he tolerate the intensity of such an ecstasy when faced with it. God could have created a being exactly like himself of course; already capable of recognising and appreciating all these and also, tolerating the intensity of those experiences but, such an action would have been self-indulgence. So, he created human beings, already armed with inner self (soul), conscience and intuitive mind (as well as the rational mind) capable of developing, evolving and climbing to higher spiritual levels with his free will. Of course, if he could recognise his mission on Planet Earth in the first place. God provided all the polar opposites within and around us on earth which together with free will are definitively the most important features of his design, especially in relation to mission which is the subject of present chapter.   According to God's plan, there have to be diversities and imperfections on this planet.   Also, as stated earlier, although all these pleasures in worldly life are shallow and short lived, but, without first experiencing them on much inferior levels in materialistic life and without learning to tolerate their lesser strength, one could not be prepared for real ones with all their strength and intensity.

*

Man starts his earthly life with two extremely opposing selves in his being.   One is the apparent self, (which is also called ego or false, physical, material, phenomenal, ephemeral, animal or lower self); pulling him to his animalistic side of the being, largely to satisfy his animal impulses.   And the other is his inner self, (also called Divine, true or real self); leading him towards the humanity.   As I expressed earlier I believe that, in the process of universal evolution when man was about to emerge on earth, God donated to him an infinitesimal fraction of his own being (spirit) in order to establish his inner self. That fraction of God's Spirit is of course infinitesimal (in comparison with the Holy Spirit) but with our understanding it is bigger than the entire universe. And it is this gift that has passed to all humans through genes and has given life to billions of individuals, without any loss or changes in its quantity and quality and will continue to do so, generation after generation. As for my belief that, the inner self, already armed with intuitive mind and conscience, is indeed the direct route of communication and connection with God; I must explain a couple of points. When I was a medical student, heavily engaged in studying basic science, especially biology and biochemistry, I came to believe that (soul) is within the molecule of (DNA) and based on the information given to me (that after physical death, molecules of DNA survive for a long period of time), I thought that, I had discovered satisfactory answers to some of my questions. For example, it ought to be the reason why (as some people believe) dead relatives and friends are aware of our presence, when we visit their graves and talk to them in silence; simply because their soul is right there among the molecules of DNA, seeing and feeling our presence. Of course, as far as I know the idea of soul residing in the DNA has not been mentioned anywhere and being a layman in such a field I found no way to reject or confirm it but I must say that it certainly provided satisfactory explanations for a few more questions such as Heaven and Hell that I referred to earlier. The other point is that in my view, apart from perfect beauty and love whose natures are difficult to define and identify, the soul and energy are most mysterious and truly the most puzzling matters for human beings to understand. Both soul and energy are from God's own being and both of these mysterious things are; not only means of communication with him but also the exact reason why he is aware of everything in entire universe all the time because a part of him either in the form of energy or soul (or both), is in everything. But when I say so, I don't mean that I comprehend or truly believe in the metaphysical Monism or Pantheism for that matter. Of course, the fact is that God manifests himself through the order of the entire universe and through the light, beauty and sublimity of nature, and we could identify nothing in the universe that does not have energy, soul or both. However, in my view the assumption that energy and soul are from God and, either one or both are in everything in nature should not lead to the ideas that "Everything is God or God exists in everything". Man of course, is an exception (due to Divine self in him) even though it may again mean that we are anthropocentric, and perhaps we are. Nevertheless, having believed that behind the appearance of matter and indeed behind all the movements is energy, without which there would be no existence in the entire universe. I wondered that; if we could comprehend the nature of energy we could probably understand everything else too.

Now returning to the main subject; if one accepts that the inner self is part of God's soul then, it becomes easy to understand why the majority of theist philosophers and all mystics of various religions believed and preached that God exists within us. It says in the Quran "God is closer to you than the artery on your neck." And Jesus Christ says, "Behold, the kingdom of God is within you." (Luke 17.20 - 21). And by referring to God as his father, Jesus declares, "He is already in you." Of course, or at least in my opinion, God does not need to be king or have a kingdom; it is simply the way most prophets taught the people, using names, terms and descriptions from the worldly lives to make it comprehensible for them. Also, any reference to God as father is symbolic and refers to presence of God's spirit in us which in that sense, and because he created us, we are all his children. However, the Eternal Self is God from which, human's inner self has temporarily been separated and to which it is destined to return. Teachings of Jesus Christ imply this very point and, Islamic

265

teachings clearly declare that too; "We are from God and to whom we return." The great poet and Sufi mystic of Persia Jalal-addin-Molavi who was born about 800 years ago (and in west is known as Rumi), dedicated the entire book of Masnavi with more than 25000 poetic couplets in it as well as mystically romantic book of (Shams-e-Tabrizi); to the love of God and longing of **(soul)** to return and re-join her origin, which is **(God)**. Notice that I just referred to the soul as her (not for the first time), and throughout this book I've referred to God as he, his or him. Choosing these pronouns for God, soul or inner self has happened subconsciously, I presume to follow the tradition. Indeed, if it were practical at all, it would be better not to allocate such pronouns; as God, soul or inner self are neither of them or perhaps all of them at the same time.

In a materialistic life, the inner self is under powerful grasp, temptations and influences of one's physical self, but she has the sacred gifts such as intuitive mind and conscience, (as well as the rational mind of course) at her disposal to work out the plan for her development and evolution using free will appropriately. And that is the first step both in understanding and fulfilling the mission. In other words, as it was touched upon earlier, man's mission requires him to distance himself from his animal impulses and instincts, from his lower self and from his animalistic side as a whole, so that, by choosing virtues in all his thoughts and deeds he could empower his inner self and develop humanity side of his existence. The fact is that man's physical self is the survival of lower stages of natural evolution, and the essence of man's mission is to eradicate this surviving element and purify himself in humanity. It is the purpose of creation that man is made with a mixture of perfection and imperfection and his mission is; to evolve and proceed towards perfection and become a perfect human. So, the mission is to develop and evolve ahead of universal evolution. The mission is to climb the ladder and arrive at the highest spiritual level. Saadi, one of the greatest poets of Persia says, "Man can reach a level, where he sees nothing but the God." Yes, our destiny is to elevate to a level, where one would see nothing but absolute beauty and, one would feel nothing but absolute peace and real love. A level at which, one experiences nothing but ineffable ecstasy and infinite happiness; the happiness that God wished to present to (others) and we are those (others) if there is no other living creature with qualities to receive it. The mission is to acquire the Real Knowledge, to find the Truth, to know God and to discover the secrets of his creation. The mission for man is to continue with his personal evolution and finally (as a perfect human), achieve the highest possible attainment which is the union with his origin; God.

*

Once I thought about the highest levels of personal development or the perfection of human beings and finally about his union with their origin, inevitably I had entered the world of Mysticism. I had entered a mysterious world that is simply too difficult to describe in ordinary words and language. I had entered a world that even the greatest mystics have found almost impossible to explain the knowledge attained or describe experiences that they encounter. Obviously, I've neither the intention nor the ability to discuss Mysticism in detail (or even in general terms) nor to describe its various formats and methods which are present in main religions. However, some introductory comments and explanations are needed in order to proceed with the current narrative. Of course, most religions have their own scope of Mysticism but perhaps it is more recognised and advanced in Hinduism, Christianity and Islam. Throughout human history various methods of self-development, moving towards the perfection and merging with the source, have been thought of, described, tried and practiced with different degrees of achievement in climbing the mountain, going up the ladder or rope (as metaphorically described by mystics) leading to God.

In Searching God

In the literature of Mysticism one usually finds many descriptions of the visions that Christian mystics have experienced, and equally various stories and visions from Sufi mystics of Islam that are recorded and offer some clarity, light and insight into the meaning of Mysticism. In some of these books though, there are technical explanations too. I would try neither of these methods at this point and hope that it would be sufficient to only bring a few examples of what mystics themselves have said. This I hope would pave the way so that I might be able to express my own understanding of Mysticism and path to perfection. I will then briefly refer to technicalities too. But before proceeding with either, I would like to add to what I have already said about the mission and about subjects such as separation of soul from the source and her longing to return and merge with her origin. I have no doubt at all that, every single one of us has occasionally felt an unexplainable loneliness (without actually being alone), a profound sorrow (without any cause for it) an unhappy sense of separation from something or someone (without having any clue from what or whom) and, a genuine longing for reunion and merger (without having slightest idea, merger with whom or what). I believe that those occasions are when inner self is crying for help and calling for the action, if we have not yet begun our long spiritual journey and path to perfection. Islam teaches that, "Man is created for man's self- development. Man is created to attain his high destiny. He was provided with the opportunity to rise to ever higher levels, and this is in God's universal plan." And this is the philosophy which is reflected in teachings of Christianity too. Throughout the history of humanity, the majority of philosophers and ideologists (if not all), have thought and wished to fulfil the mission and some have even attempted to attain the enlightenment, illumination, perfection and unification. They have also described their methods and ways of doing so. Of course, not all of them succeeded in their pursuance and not all the methods were correct. But there are striking similarities, between their methods and descriptions of the stages of path to perfection. Now, after a brief introduction I bring examples of mystics' own words (with no specific order). The important thing is the meaning of mystics' words not the person, although I will occasionally say something about whom I am quoting from.

Mysticism is strange for the majority of people and it is extremely difficult for them to understand. What true mystics experience and the real knowledge they acquire is virtually impossible to put into the words. So when they try to do so, a subject that was already difficult and complex, becomes even more perplexing (for people) and almost impossible to comprehend and appreciate. Mysticism is described as a direct consciousness of the Divine and unseen world when the veil is lifted from man's eyes. It is said that, mystics look at the higher reality and are reborn. Unless we dismiss it all as pure delusion; experiences of the mystics make it impossible to believe that, the rational consciousness is the only form of consciousness. It is said that, "Mystics experience the presence of God and enter into a glorious life. The characteristics of this life in the invisible universe are real love, a sense of freedom, an absolute peace, quickening of the intellect and, feeling of the felicity, which is not just the happiness as the word conceives it in the materialistic life, but something far more profound. And these phenomena are so real that, the physical world grows pale and becomes unstable beside them." Sufis say, "Turn to your heart and your heart will find God within itself. The problem is that, you see and feel nothing of God because you seek him outside, looking outward or try to find him in books, in a debate, in churches or at outward exercises. You will not find him there until you have first found him in your heart, in your inner self and in deepest and most central part of your soul." Al-Ghazzali, the great Sufi says, "The world is a masterpiece; he who studies it loves its invisible author in a manner that cannot be described." He says, "The love of God is the highest of our soul's progress." "When your heart has been purified," say the Sufis, "The eye of your heart opens and that eye; sees the beloved, in every person, in every blade of grass and the shining of shining in every event and every action." It is said that, "Human beings burn to find the secret of the universe." And, "The quest of man and search for the Ultimate Truth (that lies hidden beyond all the partial truth, all polar opposites and perceptions); is not a vain one." Mystics say, "To know, (as man does in a materialistic world) and to understand, (as he does with his rational mind) are not enough because; deep spirit of humanity craves for something more, something that has been given many different names such as salvation, redemption, eternal life, kingdom of the heaven and union with God."

Although man has chosen a metaphorical title drawn from the world of sense and has applied them to the nature of God, and although man has made intellectual and material images of God, when a mystic speaks of him; we hear something different from the ordinary expressions. "Nor is he a body, nor has he a form or shape, nor weight or quantity, nor is he visible or a tangible existence." As I said earlier, it is almost impossible to describe precise nature of the experiences, knowledge and visions of the mystics with the words that we use for earthly subjects and ordinary experiences and the higher they ascend the harder it becomes to do so. "As one elevates to higher and higher levels, his expressions of what he sees and knows becomes very limited, which would lead to absolute silence if he climbs any further." Rumi has repeatedly referred to this point in his poems, not only to highlight this difficulty, (which all mystics face) but also, to warn us of the burning effects of those revelations upon ordinary people. He says, "I only told you the summary and did not disclose the 'whole' had I done so both the lips and mouth would have been burnt by the flame." Many times in his poems (while he is talking at the highest level of Mysticism) Rumi abruptly becomes silent which implies; from that moment onwards no more could be put into the words. "All begins from God and ends in him, like the motion that begins from rest and ends in the rest." Mystics say, "Unless you believe; you shall not understand." And, "It is man's destiny to attain the perfection." I wonder if Pandit Nehru meant this destiny when he uttered, "We have tryst with destiny." Mystics also declare, "Deity is the noblest act of the human mind and the chief ingredient in deity is love." "We all have an idea of perfection because if we had not; we would not have known ourselves (and all that we see and experience), to be imperfect and, this comes from perfection itself which is God." "What you see as earthly splendours and beauties are only images, traces and shadows, and if you run after the trace and shadows, clinging to such beauties, you will sink down into the darkest depth of your being, where you could see or find no true light, beauty or love." "Our desires, fears and perceptions; befog our mind's mirror, cloud our mental vision and prevent us from lucidly seeing and understanding the realities. So, we must rid

276

ourselves of these distorting elements and permit the light of reality to shine directly through to us." Earlier in this book, I talked about the mirror and mystic Cup of Jam that we all possess. Here is a saying from the mystics about that point; "The mirror of heart and the fount of knowledge through it, are without limit." As Sufis and other mystics have taught us, "There are other powers and realms that you know not and, they are hidden from you." And, "To love a real human is to see the face of God." "Truly, birth marks not the beginning but a stage in life's journey and death is not an end to that journey but continuation." "The eye with which I see God is the same as that, with which, he sees me."

However it is true to say that, I had now arrived at the most significant milestone of my spiritual journey, where I had no doubt at all about the purpose of God's creation and the very fact that we have indeed a mission to fulfil. I found Mysticism one way to fulfil the mission, and I was profoundly impressed and influenced by the thoughts of the greatest mystics but perhaps mostly by Rumi, this extraordinary human, a truly ingenious poet, philosopher and a great Sufi, who died in his false selfhood to live in the Divine self and as a climber of the mountain leading to God he reached the summit. Prior to this stage of the journey, I had already envisaged the reasons why we were not created as perfect creatures, right from the beginning. Why in our earthly lives, we have to face all the rights and wrongs and, why we have to experience the beauty, love and happiness (in their ephemeral and partial forms) in this world. And finally, why we have to first develop, evolve and elevate higher in spiritual world, before being capable of tolerating the intensity of perfect happiness when we face it. At the same time I had come to the certainty (far more than just imagining) that, not only God's <u>creation</u> is continuous but he continues with universal <u>evolution</u> too. One day, (say in millions or billions years of time) an ultimate creature will reach to God's intended perfection and consciously will return to his origin to merge with. And it is this perfect creature that would see absolute beauty, feel the pure love and enjoy the infinite felicity, forever. I have no idea, nor could anyone else have, as to whether the universal evolution according to his design, would lead to the perfection of human beings or to the emergence of another creature. Of course, I hope for the former possibility to be the outcome of evolution. As I have said before; I do believe that God has given humans the opportunity to develop and reach the stage of perfection, well before the universal evolution leads to that end. And that is the purpose of creation of man that is reflected in this statement from the great Sufi poet Tarif, "The cause of creation is (perfect beauty) and (love) is the first creation". Moslems believe that God said to Prophet Mohammad, "If you did not exist, I would not have created the world." I believe true meaning of this sentence is much wider than it first appears. To me it means, if it were not for the possibility of humans developing and becoming perfect; God would not have created the universe.   That statement about Mohammad applies to anyone who has reached or will reach to that perfection. It means that God's creation was because of that possibility of perfection and because of those perfect humans; such as Jesus Christ, Prophet Mohammad and all men and women who have reached the summit or will reach it.   Perhaps countries known as superpowers and their equally powerful allies, with their inhumane and bloodthirsty leaders, with their weapons of mass destruction and their highly modern technologies; will ruin the entire civilisation and destroy the Planet Earth.   Or, as someone has said, water deficit may bring us to our knees, well before the global warming cooks us, but I universal evolution will lead to what is in God's plan, regardless. The bitter reality is that we can neither envisage the beginning with certainty nor can we have any idea about the end.   Having said so, I cannot help but dream of perfect happiness and absolute peace that man could attain if he could ascend to the highest level and acquire most essential knowledge that, as mystics say is the "knowledge of God and nature of soul", and I wonder if I could add knowledge about the energy to that phrase? Mystics believe that our findings and information are only partial knowledge and not the real one, and it is only the real knowledge that could bring ultimate satisfaction and together with the perfect beauty, provide an infinite happiness and peace for human beings.

*

Now, how do we develop ourselves and truly, how do we fulfil this mission in order to meet our destiny? These are most fundamental questions that appear to have more than one answer, considering what great mystics say of this central question, which for some would seem no answer at all. To tell the truth, a major part of my confusion was from finding too many different schools or methods of guidance that, had been offered to the shaky and hesitant beginner like me, who after reading the philosophical, theological and mystical books had

281

wondered how one could develop? Indeed there were too many ways to pursue the path of perfection. Having said that, precisely like the main religions, the essence of the doctrines are the same but their appearances and form are different. As Rumi says, "The lamps are different, the light is the same." All mystics talk about different stages of the development and elevation and virtually all begin with purification. Most of them talk about death of egocentric life and death of false self. Some mystics divide the stages to purgation, illumination and unification. Others describe these stages of mystic way to perfection as active life (with or without illumination), interior life (inward man) and super-essential life (God seeing life). Some of the mystics name and describe these stages rather differently; talking about purification, concentration, and identification. It seems that in all mystic schools (or at least in the way of Sufi) the crucial step is getting rid of the animal self, a complete death of false selfhood and of course, the ultimate goal is unification with our origin - God. In this very point, I found astonishing similarities between the Mysticism within Catholic Theology and Sufi Mysticism within Islam. I learned that Mysticism is not a doctrine confined to Christianity or Islam. In fact, purifying the self and strive for enlightenment, illumination and experiencing the Nirvana already existed in Hinduism and Buddhism. In Zoroastrianism, the central aspect of teachings is about righteousness, right thinking, purity of mind, right speaking and right actions, which is not too far away from the purification mystics are talking of. In Buddhism, the stages of development are: 'sila' (morality) which is abstaining from unwholesome deeds of the body and speech, then 'samadhi' (mastery over one's mind) that is right effort, mindfulness, awareness, concentration and finally, 'Panna' (wisdom) that is to say purifying the mind that leads to the right thought and right understanding.   Attar, one of the greatest Sufi mystics, divided the journey of man towards perfection to seven valleys; Valley of Quest, (to search and strip away the obstacles), Valley of Love (first stage of illumination), Valley of Knowledge and Enlightenment (God is seen in everything), Valley of Detachment, (when soul is utterly absorbed in the Divine love), Valley of Unity (when vision of God is transient), Valley of Bewilderment (light is too bright, soul is dazzled but, one is ready for the next stage) and finally Valley of Annihilation (where selfhood disappears and one merges with God).   Other Sufi mystics have described these stages with different names and forms but in all, the essence remains just the same which is the direct love of God, direct inner experiences and direct vision of Divine nature of reality and all end in; total annihilation and complete death of the false self, pure peace and union with the Beloved.   Sufis call this final stage of the spiritual attainment 'bagha', which is dwelling in the living presence of God, in constant knowledge of his secrets and, in total merger with the source.   However, what is absolutely clear to me is that, nothing can be achieved while one remains in the prison of his false self.   As the mystics say; "By killing your false self you will regain your true self." Or, "One must die in his animal selfhood and be born again." And, "If you are not dead to self and detached from all earthly things, do not expect to see the light." "In the way of perfection and unification with God the abandonment of everything even one's own selfhood, is the key."

The other point that was perfectly clear to me was that, merely the love of God could save us from succumbing to our animal selves. Mystics persistently talk about the love and wine. If we do not comprehend what they mean by love and wine, it might seem to us that, they have nothing worth talking about except for drunkenness and lust. It is equally important to appreciate how they refer to love of God in their poems and speeches. As mystics find it difficult to express the intensity of their love to God, they use the ordinary words and terms. Whenever a mystic (especially Sufi mystic) refers to the wine he means mystic wine, sacred wine, wine of the gnosis and bliss and by referring to love, he means love of God even though, in their poems it may sound as if they are addressing beautiful women. But here, beloved is God himself. Rumi describes these points beautifully; "Die in love, if you want to remain alive. The creed and denomination of love is God. If you have not been the lover of God, do not count your life as lived." He then emphasises the point by adding; "On the day of reckoning it will not be counted." He says, "However drunk the wine made me yesterday, today his wine is drunk in me." Rumi wants to help man (as the lover) merge with the Beloved and to return him to his origin. Rumi wants to unite the part with the whole and return the drop of water to ocean from which, it has been separated. Love of God is the cornerstone of Mysticism and time comes when; the mystic is at once the love, the lover, and the Beloved. At this stage the mystic is so absorbed and merges with the Divine, he finds no difference between his perfected self and God. This stage and such station cannot be expressed in words and, if the mystic attempts to do so, he might say, "I am the Truth." Or, "Glory to me how great is my glory." And, that was what happened to Hallaj, the great Sufi mystics of Islam who lost his head for supposed blasphemy.

*

I am conscious that the world of Mysticism whether in Hinduism, Christianity, Islam or any other religion is an ocean and what I have said is merely a drop, but at least I have tried to illustrate a passage of the journey, which was the most fascinating and awakening stage. One important fact I have learned for certain is that, the death of (false self) is the prime requirement for higher levels of development and evolution; if one wishes to climb the ladder leading to God. I learned that one must break the wall, free his Divine self from the prison of false self, and be born again while he lives. In relation to this essential point in one's development and evolution, Rumi's son (Sultan Valad), expresses his father's thoughts in these words.

287

"Man must be born twice, once from his mother and next from his own body and his own existence.   The body is like an egg and the essence of man must become a bird in that egg through the warmth of love and then he can escape from his body and fly in the eternal world of the soul beyond time and space."   The first birth happens to all of us naturally, when we are freed from that dark prison of womb, but the second birth and escape from the prison of false selves, would happen if only we were willing as well as capable of breaking the walls and escape, which is what mystics mean; when they talk about being borne again.   Rumi's books are saturated with poems regarding the breaking down prison walls, breaking from the cage to fly, annihilating the ego, loving God, and returning to him to merge. In fact, his book of Masnavi begins with poems about reed (Ney in Persian language) and, how its melancholic music complains of the separation from its source (reed bed), and bitterly longs for the union. I wish that the readers could study his poems in original language (Farsi).   Unfortunately, all the available translations fail to do justice to the thoughts of this great poet. They fail to show his ingenuity or convey his messages to human beings. However, all mystics have often referred to annihilation of false selfhood and, death of egocentric life as the most important chapter in one's development, evolution and path to perfection. Jesus said, "Except a man was born again he cannot see the kingdom of God." He also said, "Unless a man be regenerated in the spirit of mind, have his will and affections transferred from earthly to spiritual objects; he cannot see the kingdom of God."

*

So, having appreciated that our mission is a long journey in the path to perfection I asked how, do we get there? How do we develop, climb the ladder, and elevate? Then I studied and contemplated the variety of ways described, some of them totally unacceptable to my understandings of the whole matter. I found the Sufi way, the Mysticism of love, immensely fascinating and became very much affected by the poems of Rumi and his thoughts. But I also realised that, exactly like the religions, Mysticism has been corrupted and misused, as I will try to explain in following chapter. However, the intellectuals of Café Naderi ridiculed all the matters that I had discussed in our meetings, more and less as I have described here. They dismissed them categorically and said, "What are these false(s) and true(s) in all your nonsense? What do you mean by true love and real happiness? We have lots of love and happiness and they seem quite real to us. We actually feel them with all our natural senses. Why should we abandon all these pleasures and happiness that we already have and begin probing for different types that; we can neither see, nor feel, nor prove that they exist? We already have plenty of everything, food, wine, music, dance, sex, luxury and many more, which make us happy. What else do you want? Do you honestly want to leave all the beautiful things that you can see, feel, and touch in this life and climb up your hypothetical ladder or rope to find absolute beauty. Are you crazy? Are you

really serious in trying to find a true happiness that you hope;

will be generated in you, the moment you reached to God and

saw his lovely image? Are you out of your mind?"

How could one answer these questions? I asked myself.

How could one explain a reality that cannot be seen or felt, in

an ordinary way?   How could you convince someone who

already feels quite happy and truly content that; there is a real

happiness well above what he has experienced from earthly

pleasures?   Immersed in their hedonistic and sybaritic lives

they say, "We are happy with what we have, thank you very

much." How can one argue with that?   Of course, if they had

liberated their inner selves and empowered them; it would be a

different matter.   Had their conscience woken up to be

ashamed of submerging in the animalistic side of their beings,

there could be a chance to understand the merits of being a real

human being. Had they seen pure light and perfect beauty

radiating from a spiritually elevated person, there could be still some hope of the rehabilitation and rescue.   But I'm afraid I had become just as disappointed in the Intellectuals of Café Naderi as they were in me. In their view I had utterly regressed.   Signs of regression were evident in every single word that I uttered and could not be hidden from them.   And in any case, the extent of my regrettable degeneration was (in their opinion) incurable. But I continued with my search to find answers to my questions, regardless.

Chapter 13

Fulfilment of the Mission

So, on Planet Earth there is a "mission" for human beings and the essence of their mission is to achieve perfection, is that true? I asked myself again and again. That is to say; one ought to develop, evolve and elevate to higher levels and become a perfect human, in order to obtain the real knowledge and unravel the secrets of God's creation. And then, one would return to one's origin to merge with and behold the ineffable beauty, experience the true love and live in absolute peace and infinite felicity forever. Okay, but how we could fulfil the mission? I wondered. Do we all leave everything aside and become ascetics or recluses? Do we find a Buddha Tree, sit under its comforting shadow and do nothing but contemplate and wait for the sudden enlightenment? Do we have to follow a religion or believe in existence of God in order to develop? Could we not succeed in personal development and advancement of our humanity through a mere belief in humanism? Whatever method and doctrine we choose to follow, would we need a master or a saint to take our hands and show us the way? Could we not do it with our own efforts? There were many more questions in my mind that needed clarification. But at least, one thing was quite clear to me that; simply believing in the morality and righteousness without taking any action would not get us anywhere. Simply admitting that; there is a mission for man to develop and evolve towards perfection, without making any effort has no value at all and would not lead to a spiritual elevation. Mere acquaintance with the variety of methods to fulfil this task will not help us either. Even teaching on mystic methods of development, or as an authority, lecturing or writing books on spirituality and metaphysical topics, without taking any practical step; will not bear fruits either. And what do we mean by practical steps, I asked myself? Are asceticism, austerity and rigid abstinence or self-denial the types of practical steps that we need to take? Do these practical steps include self-harm, mortification and solitary living, by shutting the door to outside world? Is total denial of the worldly things a practical step? No, I did not think that I could accept these notions. I did not see, and could not accept that such bizarre actions would on their own, lead to enlightenment and perfection. Of course, in ascending the ladder, climbing the mountain or rope leading to God, a stage could arrive at which earthly things or partial pleasures become nothing for the person. Surly at such a level there is total detachment from the animal desires of false self and from all the earthly pleasures. But by no means, will one develop and ascend the ladder merely by depriving himself from everything and choosing to isolate himself in a corner. By no means could one achieve anything on the spiritual journey simply by denying the natural necessities for normal life and harming his physical health, whilst doing nothing useful for his people and his community. I strongly believe that, any step to personal development and evolution, and any effort made for fulfilling of such a mission should be taken whilst one is living a normal life amongst other people within a community. One should take these steps while working hard for his living and attend to his personal care and maintain his physical and mental health. He should do so, while he fulfils his responsibilities to his loved ones as well as fellow countrymen and indeed, human race at large. In fact, a true master and genuine mystic, lives in the midst of other people, not in isolation and definitely, not in a palace or in an ivory tower. Therefore, we need actions and practical steps, bearing in mind those conditions and not just the words; I concluded.

Years ago, I read a book written by a religious man. He had described the most bizarre methods, for spiritual elevation, enlightenment and unification with God from which I remember a few things such as; using dreams and hallucinations and nonstop praying or constant recitation of God's attributes and even using narcotic drugs. I did not keep the book in my library and can't remember the name of the author or the title of his book. But, the methods suggested in such books seems to me; inducing the illumination, enlightenment and love of God, artificially and forcefully. I could not agree with these methods.

*

However as the true mystics have described, there are some practical steps that can be taken if the traveller of such a spiritual journey takes his mission and destiny seriously, and if he truly wishes to rise above his false self and animalism. The primary steps in my view, are nothing more than or different from what most people take for self-improvement and we refer to them as "good persons". Although I strongly believe that majority of these ordinary "good persons" are religious people and that they respect moral values and righteousness because of their religious beliefs or fear of God, but faith in any religion or even theism; <u>are not essential for the first steps at this phase of the development</u>.   Many nonbelievers also have excellent characters.   In fact, the first few steps of development have nothing to do with Mysticism either.   I asked myself, is it not true to say that secular humanism is the rejection of religions in favour of belief in advancement of the humanity by its own effort?   Is it not also true to say that there are many humanists with excellent characters who we often meet and respect as righteous and virtuous individuals even though, some of them do not believe in God?   Yes it is true, and we all have met and respected them. But practical problem here is that any further advancement towards perfection, if that is indeed their target and destination, would not be possible, whilst their ego-centrism and their overriding false selves continue to exist.

The fact is that, without higher motivations; it is almost impossible to overcome such dominance.   That is precisely why; at the higher levels of self–development, not only the belief in God but also loving him becomes absolute necessities for the path to perfection. And it is exactly at the higher levels that difficulties begin to manifest and practically very few of the climbers could continue and reach the summit.   As far as I could understand the journey towards perfection begins by simply attempting to become a good person and acquire good character. It could start from observing and respecting moral values.   It could start from the practicing virtues and from not harming others, not lying and not stealing.   In other words it can start by just pursuing and practicing what Zoroaster and Guatama taught; which are right thoughts, right words and right deeds.   Once such a "good person" avoided acting immorally or illegally and once all his works and labours were focused on caring and supporting his loved ones he is ready to progress.   Once he begins assisting others without expecting

299

anything in return, and once he experiences genuine satisfaction and pleasure from serving people it is only then that he would be ready to take the next steps. And the next steps begin from liberating and empowering one's inner self to overcome his false self. I honestly believe that the moment that, one finds his real self and tries to free her from the prison of false self, he also becomes certain without any doubt in his mind that there are other things in life beside the partial, empty and short-lived earthly pleasures and there is a purpose behind the presence of human on this planet. And at this level of development, life seems more serious and one contemplates the mysteries of life more deeply and for a much longer period of time, while worldly pleasures appear far more transient and empty.

*

As an ordinary person, I have used ordinary words and phrases, to outline my limited understanding of the mission, stages of the journey, and steps that ought to be taken in practical terms and I do apologise for too much simplicity. However, I believe the next practical steps are very difficult and that is exactly why most people who have developed thus far, are stuck at this stage of development, if at all they were lucky and did not descend to the inferior levels. In fact most of the mystics believe that, if one is not yet ready to take the next crucial steps and he is not prepared to climb higher up the ladder, the consequences of further efforts could turn out to be disastrous, and the person may fall into an hedonistic life far worse than that which he had at the start of the journey. And if this happens he might succumb to his animal self and even deny and ridicule all his beliefs in spirituality that encouraged him to begin the quest, in the first place. I will return to the next steps of the path to perfection but first, it is appropriate to refer to certain realities of life as I see them. It is a reality that the majority of ordinary people live with righteousness and virtues and have respect for moral values but they do not bother about the mission of humans on earth nor do they completely surrender to their animal demands and false selfhoods. The remaining minority go to two extreme directions. That is to say; either they begin a long spiritual journey in order to develop, reach higher levels and climb further up the mountain towards the summit or, they drown in the depths of their hedonistic life and live like the animals. It is this latter group of people who are behind all our sufferings. Truly, those who succumb to their animal natures and consciously, with free will, choose evil deeds and wickedness; will remain in their animalistic life and never develop to see the light or attain real knowledge and experience the true love and felicity. These people were in the past, are at the present time, and will be in the future the perpetrators of crimes in human societies. We have seen and known many ordinary people of the latter group who have committed sins, atrocities and crimes on a relatively lesser scale, as well as the vast number of tyrants (such as kings, prime ministers, presidents and even religious leaders), who have disgracefully committed unbelievable brutalities, crimes and wickedness, <u>on a larger scale</u>. The content of history books and news of current events as we hear in media, confirms a bitter realities that, these humanlike beasts in power, have savagely persecuted, robbed, burnt, tortured and raped countless innocent and helpless people and have been responsible for all the wars, destructions and genocides.   These are a disgrace to humanity and are precisely the people who did not, do not and will not exert themselves to rise above the beast and live nobly by any means.   So, in real life and practically few people begin the spiritual voyages and try to climb the mountain leading to God and fewer still reach the summit. Some succumb to their animal natures and totally immerse themselves in hedonistic lives, and these are behind all the atrocities against humanity. But the majority are ordinary people and they possess good characters whether or not they believe in any religion or God. This point is reflected in the following expressions from mystics. "Some immerse in the material world, earthly needs and demands. Others rise above it." And, "People who let the animal qualities determine their conducts eventually become like the beasts." The reality is that, these are the very people who cannot find their real selves in order to release from the prison of false self and even if they find and make an effort to release the real selves, their wickedness, their evil thoughts and their evil actions will surly weaken and undermine their efforts. And that is precisely the point that mystics refer to; "As a result of excessively pursuing their animal desires, their inner selves might be pushed to the edge of being destroyed or blinded." And, "Indeed the voice of the conscience might stop, as a result of false principles and self-deceiving reasoning."

Finding one's real self and liberating her from the dark prison of false self will not happen overnight; it is a gradual process and is attained progressively. It is true to say that unconditional service to people and help to those in need would certainly accelerate the process. Being at the service of people is an extremely significant step to take, but it never helps, if one does it for something in return and, in hope of reward, accolade and fame. The more one serves others, without expecting rewards in return, the stronger the inner self becomes. Charity is equally important step in one's self-development but again, this will only yield fruits if it was done without showing off, and without having other purposes in one's mind such as; tax exemptions, honours, celebrity or even acquisition of a good name. Charity ought to be of things that still have some value to the owner and one is aware that it is still useful for oneself, not just from unwanted and disliked items. It should be done in such a way that even the receivers do not know from whence they came let alone informing the whole nation. Giving service to people in the best possible manner and with readiness, pleasure and humility without any expectation will definitely weaken the false self and empower the inner self. The same is true for participating in works of charity, which one should do in a manner described above. It is at this stage of the spiritual journey and at this level of development and evolution that through the mirror within his inner self, one would see things which had never entered into his mind and it is here that one becomes even more resolute to fortify his inner self; in order to purify himself further and amend the imperfections in his being. And this is exactly the stage that one faces the most difficult steps to take; the destruction of animalistic aspects of one's being and detachment from the earthly things. Although these steps are really difficult to take, sincere travellers are not left alone, there is help, I understand. That is to say; all of us, whether we are believers or not, have an image of God within us that can neither be seen with sufficient clarity nor be described in ordinary words, and it is precisely this image that comes to assist one to take those final difficult steps. Mystics call this stage "Consciousness of God-image in the soul." At this phase

306

of the evolution, the clouded mirror is cleaned and cleared up, and the traveller sees the light and has clearer vision of that image in his real self. And it is at this level that he gets a glimpse of absolute beauty and senses the perfect love such that he has never felt before. It is indeed the love of that image, love of God and love of absolute beauty that makes the next steps much easier to take and accelerates the spiritual ascension. But one could not be prepared for this real love unless he loves other human beings as clearly expressed by a mystic; "If a man loves not his brother whom he has seen, how can he love God whom he has not seen?"

*

I confess that topics such as renunciation of worldly pleasures and the annihilation of the animal self are immensely difficult subjects for me to discuss seriously. Because on the one hand, I can understand that as part of development one should distance oneself from excessive worldly pleasures and,

307

be prepared to say no, to animal cravings.   But on the other hand, I cannot accept that the austerity or asceticism and similar methods on their own could be an effective means for self-development and evolution without other efforts and undertakings that I have referred to earlier. I believe that God created all necessities and earthly pleasures for a purpose. With free will, we must choose the ones that are good and useful for our body and mind and avoid the ones that are not. They are not provided on earth to be totally ignored or abstained.   They are in fact vital for continuation of the healthy life and for provision of opportunities; to pursue our mission on this planet and meet our destiny.   The difficulty arises from misunderstanding and misinterpretation of the reasons why we are here.   We are not here, I thought, for earthly things and pleasures it is indeed the other way around. They are here because of our mission and destiny.   They are here for our individual evolution, elevation and perfection.   I often expressed this point, during debates with infidel and atheist intellectuals that; we eat to live, we don't live to eat. I used "eating" as an example, because it is easy to appreciate the point I wanted to make but the same is true for anything else.   In other words, our mentality should change and we should acknowledge that, they have been provided on earth, so that life could continue generation after generation and evolution advances to its culmination.

The ascetic life, abstinence or total renunciation of provisions and earthly pleasures are just as much wrong as living a sybaritic and hedonistic life.   In my view a minimum of earthly provisions and other natural gifts are needed for a healthy and normal life so that we have the opportunities to progress in our quest, to unravel the secrets of universe and acquire real knowledge.   We should enjoy the provisions in moderation and only to the extent that is necessary in order to have basic means for continuation of the journey.   I thought in this way, one could conquer one's false self and egocentrism, detach oneself from excessive materialistic pleasures and be born again in one's real self. Of course, as one ascends to higher and higher levels, one's false self becomes weaker and weaker, which may eventually lead to its complete disappearance. Mystics express this as follow; "Killing of the false self while we live." "Burning away the ego, completely." and, "Surrendering the selfhood, and dying within oneself."

So, at the highest phase of the spiritual elevation it is the complete annihilation of animal self, it is surrender of the ego, it is the absolute detachment from worldly pleasures, it is dying in one's false self, and it is being reborn in one's Divine self. Sufi mystics believe that in the process of spiritual elevation, it is an absolute requirement to be completely detached from all earthly things and pleasures and to be indifferent to them. Once you are at such stage and level of the evolution, then you have everything. In other words, as mystics say, "When you have given up everything, everything becomes yours." which of course seems paradoxical and ironic to the layperson. In any case, very few reach to this level and culmination of their quests. Most of the travellers do not continue with their journey and that is also the reality of life that I was talking about. And why they cannot continue, one may ask. Because, when it comes to changing of one's attitude towards the reasons behind the presence of pleasures or provisions on earth, when it comes to changing of emphasis on utilising them, and finally, when it comes to detaching from earthly pleasures, certain hindrances and powerful factors prevent their continuous efforts. These factors and obstacles are; competition in a materialistic life that, together with extensive marketing propaganda, create a spending mentality and desire for a luxurious life. And this, together with the other social pressures and attractiveness of the hedonistic life; prevents further advancement in the development and continuation of the spiritual journey, a journey that does not yield instant

311

pleasure nor gains, to satisfy the traveller. The traveller suddenly realizes that he is falling behind and losing everything. He realises that, others are enjoying life in full, are far more successful in society, have gained much more fortune and have attained higher and better positions in the materialistic world, while he has achieved far less in this world, has gained nothing in his search and has reached nowhere in the other side! I have seen quite a few of these expectant travellers of spiritual journey, whom having climbed the first steps of the ladder have disastrously dropped, regressed and sadly returned to their former worldly lives, if not worse and even lower. I believe the main reason for abrupt discontinuation of journey and regression is a disappointment. It is a disappointment at the failure to achieve anything immediate or tangible, except for being regarded as good persons by the others, at the most. Also, as some of travellers expect to attain special powers and prestige, they become disappointed and frustrated at not gaining anything

312

like that! These people do not realise that, if their quest was merely their egoistical desire to acquire especial skills and power or to gain higher social status; their efforts were bound to fail right from the beginning. Indeed, any step towards the evolution and development that in reality is the hidden desire of ego for its own gains, is bound to fail badly. Even the desire to learn and acquire knowledge would get nowhere beyond gaining partial information, if it is only for want of ego, and such knowledge, most likely will be at ego's service. This point is beautifully expressed in Andrew Harvey's book of "The way of passion", where he quotes this from Rumi; "That desire to understand is the ego's desire to control; to imperialize the highest kind of knowledge for its own ends. That desire to understand is the ego's desperate attempt to pretend that it is doing the initiation that, it is initiating itself, and if it succeeds in making you to believe it, you are trapped - far more trapped in fact, thinking that you know than knowing that you don't know"

Indeed, there is another serious problem with some of the pursuers of Mysticism that ought to be mentioned before advancing any further and that is surprisingly; arrogance. Some travellers, as soon as have climbed only a few steps on the ladder; think that, they are above anyone else and have attained real knowledge and power. However, in reality their egos, having realised that such a voyage is working against the interests of false selves, use spiritual accomplishments to reinforce these travellers' selfishness, by revitalising their egocentrism, which puts an end to further progress and might even lead to regression. I've said enough about the difficulties of overcoming egocentrism and have also talked about those who fail to accomplish their tasks, and I have tried to explain why. But, what about travellers on this journey who do succeed? For those who begin their long and demanding quest in order to first become good persons then, real humans and finally, perfect humans; this is what happens. When they reach the higher levels, further progress gets easier, ascension accelerates and becomes faster. Of course, this is the case only when one's efforts are for God and his love, nothing else. Indeed once the traveller has seen the light, has a clearer "image" of God in the mirror of his inner self, has a glimpse of the inexpressible beauty and has felt the true love; he finds that, there is a magical power pulling him upwards. Unlike the beginning of the journey, when any progress or achievement can be disappointingly very slow, at the higher levels, one experiences an unexpected acceleration of the whole process, a speed which could no longer be explained only by the efforts of traveller. At this stage, the ascension towards the source is extraordinarily fast, as if a gigantic magnetic field absorbs a small piece of iron and that is indeed the power of true love, a true love without which, no one could reach the summit. That is what I've learned from the mystics, but how many people have reached that level, I have no idea.

*

What I have briefly said so far, is simply an account of my comprehension of the mission and ways of fulfilling the task. I am aware that it is too simplistic a description of an immeasurably mysterious and serious subject, but nonetheless it is part of the story and my struggles to find the Truth that had to be narrated with utmost honesty.   Now, do we really need the religions, ceremonies and rituals in order to develop, evolve, climb the ladder, and move towards the perfection? Perhaps not, I believe. I mean they are not definite necessities but it would be a great help if we were believers and had faith, would it not? Do we have to believe in God in order to evolve and become perfect human beings? Well, what should I say? Without God and his love there is no meaning to mission in the first place and there is nothing to achieve; so, of course we need to believe in God. Do we need a mystic and a so called master, to help and show us the way? I would say, certainly

<u>not</u>.   I mean not at the present market. What do I mean by market? Well, in my opinion, Mysticism exactly like religions has been misunderstood, misused and corrupted. Like religions, in some schools of Mysticism believers or disciples are more engaged in ceremonies and rituals than they are in evolution and self-development.   If a master in the past, reached the highest level in evolution, saw the absolute beauty, experienced the infinite ecstasy and at the height of bliss danced in the streets like a drunkard, it does not mean that if we too performed precisely the same dance, ritually and regularly, we would develop and reach the same level.   I don't wish to go into detail but there are many examples.   The other problem is that Mysticism has today become a profitable business and also is a way of hiding one's animalism, under the garment of false spirituality. It is now fashionable for ultra-rich persons and those who are fed up with trying the same old tools to attain earthly pleasures; to turn to spirituality. They do not take the matter seriously or implement any guidance but

rather, they turn to it to satisfy their own egos. When they are temporarily tired of repetitiveness of their hedonistic and sybaritic lives and when it appears as if, nothing in materialistic lives is left to satisfy them; they pretend to have embraced Mysticism and Spirituality. Why do they do so, one might ask? Well, on the one hand it is to show off to their peers that they are now at a higher and totally different level, when nothing new or unique in their materialistic life is left to show off about. On the other hand it is to gain a period of respite so that, having been briefly weaned from worldly pleasures, they could return to their former lives and experience the same pleasures that they did in the good old days. These people often join cults or hire personal spiritual mentors. And because there is demand in the market; inevitably there is also a mass production of masters. Some of these false masters are clever and perhaps lucky too, so, they become famous and gather numerous disciples and followers around them. Behind the curtain they live in luxury, but of course, in the eyes of the people, they conduct very simple lives as mystics. In reality, such masters are, neither truly developed nor enlightened individuals nor are their followers and disciples genuinely after the fulfilment of mission or to become better humans. Rather, both sides have something to gain from this profitable business. False masters get rich (apparently from the voluntary donations) and acquire the power to abuse their followers, whether financially, influentially or sexually and enjoy their celebrity status and the way they are worshipped. On the other side, the ultra-rich and the false travellers also get what they want which is a personal spiritual mentor among their other possessions, to show off to their associates to go along with their mansions, jewellery, expensive cars, yachts, personal trainers, masseurs, bodyguards, hairdresser, manicurist and so on. The very fact is that, when excessive indulgence in the earthly pleasures reaches a stage at which nothing pleases them anymore they suddenly remember the spiritual side of the life. One must admit that very few might genuinely wake up and truly realise that they have indeed a mission to fulfil.   But the rest just want new things to show off and a period of rest from their materialistic life, so that they can start fresh.   This is precisely like drug addicts who no longer respond to even highest doses of drugs and therefore seek assistance from health professionals in order to give up their addictions and then, start afresh from the lowest dose of drug with desired effects and satisfaction as before.   However, there is a demand for such masters of Mysticism and there are plenty of them in the market.   Many are familiar with the subject of spirituality and the mystics' way of spiritual attainment at least enough to convince the fool and some might even claim enlightenment and perfection, but in reality they have achieved neither.   Why do I say these with such certainty and confidence that could sound harsh a judgment?   Simply because I know that a true mystic, a truly developed and enlightened person would never use Mysticism to attain fame and wealth.   He or she would never live in a palace, in luxury or in an ivory tower. He or she would never abuse anyone's wealth, position or influence for own gains and satisfaction and surely would never make a business out of it. Of course, having access to the guidance of a true mystic who is close to the summit and, assistance of a genuinely enlightened master is extremely precious and very rare opportunity for the travellers of the spiritual journey and one might be fortunate to meet such a master but there are not many of them around. A true mystic lives amongst the ordinary people and lives a very simple life. Most people would not recognise him and they may even ridicule, tease and abuse him as a bizarre person, but those people who have discovered and liberated their own real selves would instantly recognise him. He will not preach, he will not teach you, he will not formally accept you as a disciple, he will not accept favours from you, whether offered voluntarily or otherwise and he might not talk much either. But, he will certainly be a great help and guide you in this journey which is the path to perfection. When you meet him and his eyes fix on you, you will remember God. No, it is more than that; not just remembering, you will see the light of God radiates through him. You will sense that God manifests himself through him and you will indeed appreciate how beautiful is the real human as he is. You will instantly fall in love with that beauty and will long to reach the source of it. In other words he will support you and assist you just with his being, with his presence. If one is lucky enough to meet a truly developed person at the highest level; any doubt about the existence of God (the main obstacle on road of journey), will vanish and the ascension towards the summit will be accelerated. And that is exactly what happened to the great mystic and poet (Rumi), when he met (Shams).

While editing this chapter I realised that I've utterly failed to describe a subject such as Mysticism in general terms and the Sufi way specifically. In my bitter disappointment and regret, I pitifully consoled myself by remembering that, the topic is difficult to put into the words anyway and I had already warned the readers of this.   Now with that self-consolation and comfort, I close this chapter but not the book yet because I must catch up with other events and describe my final convictions.   So far, it was all about ups and downs in understanding and belief, let us see; what is the result of reading books, debating with intellectuals and searching for the Truth. .

Chapter14

The final convictions

What should be the title of last chapter? I wondered. I could name it as the summary of course, as it is indeed partly the summary of what I've already said or, I could name it as the conclusion but I chose' The final convictions' and by doing so, I raised a big question. Is it really the final? Well, at this point of the time as I write these words, the answer to that crucial question is a definite yes but I also know that how vulnerable one could be when faced with insidious emergence of doubts that are generated by his false self even if it is partly controlled and dominated by the real self.   These doubts, occasionally and briefly, will continue to reappear until one's conviction is weakened, unless of course, one has reached a level that enables one to resist all temptations.

Indeed after more than half a century of searching for the Truth, inside and outside the books and after a quarter of a century of political, theological and moral debates with all kinds of intellectuals what do I believe now and what do I no longer believe?   It a fair question; what is the result of contemplating for years?   What are the final verdicts after all those fluctuations in belief as well as ups and downs in personal and social life?   What do I believe now; after going through numerous extraordinary events and experiencing different circumstances that inevitably affect one's ideologies? In last chapter of this book, I will try to answer that very question with all honesty. But first I would like to return to the Intellectuals of Café Naderi and to political activities that, we had together, alongside the spiritual journeys, in order to update the patient and loyal readers with that side of story too.

The long- awaited revolution began with the full participation of all intellectuals in that cafe, not only in street demonstrations but also in armed struggles. This was indeed a big surprise for everyone after so many years of their "empty talks", a phrase with which the working class had ridiculed and summed up contribution and political activities of intellectuals. Yes, the revolution arrived and it succeeded as Shah was overthrown. I have a fascinating inside story from that historical event and the "war" that was imposed on the nation almost immediately after the victory of revolution but that side of story will come in a separate book I hope, as such detail is beyond the scope of this current report. Therefore, I will mention only few points to conclude political side of the narration.

*

The Iranian revolution of 1978-79 has been named the third greatest revolution in the history of human race, following the French and Bolshevik revolutions. This was an all-inclusive revolution that united the whole nation, from far left to far right

327

of the political spectrum, obviously with the exception of Royalists. About a year before the revolution reached its final stage the society of Intellectuals of Café Naderi was revitalised and once again became a leading and significant centre for revolutionaries. Of course, it is an accepted fact that the main centres for preparation of final stages of struggle were mosques as revolution began by the uprising of Khomeini's followers. Many new and enthusiastic young members joined us and almost all the senior members of the group who had earlier escaped abroad returned home. They returned to join the final assault against the Shah and his notorious government and army. Surviving political prisoners were set free from the prisons and torture cells, and several of our friends were amongst them. Debates in our meetings became hotter and more serious mostly concerning political matters but obviously, religious issues could not be avoided because of the nature of revolution. In fact, after the victory of revolution, religion was the main subject of discussions if not the only one.   Interestingly, quite a few of the infidel intellectual became religious and those of the gang, who had remained non-believers, reluctantly and perhaps tactically, had accepted the leadership of the religious elites of the country. They anticipated and hoped that after the victory of revolution, the religious leaders would return to the mosques and religious schools and the intellectuals would take over the running of the country.   But that sweet hope did not materialise and as a matter of fact, the opposite turned out to be the case.   The revolution triumphed, the Shah escaped and a new regime, The Islamic Republic of Iran was founded.   Those members of our society, who had embraced Islam were rewarded by posts in the new government, or, somehow were attached to the ruling system and close to power. But the rest of gang had a difficult time that I prefer to omit this from my narrative in this book except to say that, "The Revolution eats its own children." and this revolution was not an exception. However, this was a period of the time in which, the media had been saturated by the religious debates or preaching and religious subjects were included in the agenda of all meetings at every level. It was the first time that religious leaders were actually ruling the country and their function was under constant and thorough scrutiny of the observers, both outside and within the nation.

The imposed war between Iran and Iraq created new and unforeseen circumstances that changed the direction of the movement altogether. Whether this was the intention of those who imposed the war on nations, I could not be certain. The war, mass murder and destruction, lasted for almost eight years during which, more than one million young men and women were slain, and at least two millions seriously injured and disabled. I witnessed the constructive side of religion, as well as its destructive side, depending on how the teachings were interpreted and for what purpose. I saw its beauty in pure and real form as well as its frightening ugliness in its corrupted and misleading version. I was delighted and indeed proud of the former and disappointed and ashamed of the latter. I saw how religion and religious leaders could unite the people and how different reading and interpretations of the teachings could divide them and create bitter hostilities and hatred. I saw the power of sincere faith in practice and in real life. This was no longer the reading of religious and historical books, no longer listening to stories; it was the real thing happening right before my eyes demonstrating how strong people could become with religious beliefs and faith? How easily the religious people can give everything they have, including their own lives, for what they believe to be the Truth? And how easily religious leaders could manipulate people both for good and evil purposes? However, this was the first time in the country's history that people were living in a purely religious society. It had a profound effect on some of the members of the group I was associated with, but it did not and has not changed my beliefs significantly.

*

So, that question again. What do I believe in now and what do I not believe any more?   What is my final conclusion? Indeed, I must explain this because, what I narrated in previous chapters, was based on social and political situations, the events in my personal life and the condition of the road and influence of fellow travellers with anticipated ups and downs and changes in direction.   I trust kind readers would appreciate that certain points must be repeated here to conclude. Without a shadow of doubt I believe God exists.   This conviction has got nothing to do with scientific evidence (although it is available to support that belief if one prefers scientific proof for his conviction), nor it is merely based on undeniable signs of design in everything especially in living creatures, (even though design in universe on its own is more than enough to convince any rational mind), nor it is the result of logical analysis and rationalisation. It is predominantly based on the evidence of my inner self and intuitive mind. Of course, all the other reasons were useful in debates and naturally should have had influenced my conclusion and I am sure they have. There is no god but the God and he cannot be seen by physical eyes or defined by the ordinary words that we use for the earthly matters. There is only one Truth and one God who created the entire universe. God reflects his beauty and signs of his existence through the nature, through the order and design in universe, to help us to believe in him but, he does not need to come down to earth in man's shape or any other form to prove his existence and I believe he has never done so. The proof is already within us and we can see God with inner eyes and through the mirror of the heart which we all possess but only if we succeed in freeing our Divine selves from prison of false selves and only if, we could learn to use our intuitive minds beside the rational minds. Rumi says; "Why do you weep? The source is within you." The signs, source and proof are within us why we are hesitating? What else do we want?

333

It says in the Quran, "We show them signs on the horizons and in themselves." I believe that God does not need to perform miracles either in order to prove his existence to us, because such measures are contrary to the purpose of creating the man and indeed contrary to man's mission and destiny.

I believe that any person (at any level of the society), who gives a specific name to God other than the word of God in his language or attributes a specific personality and shape to God commits big mistake if not a crime. I also believe any person at any level who suggests there is a different God for different religions and by doing so divides the nations consciously or unconsciously commits a dangerous mistake if not crime against morality and humanity. I definitely believe that the harm done to human societies by the atheist thinkers, who only debate against the existence of God, is by far less than the harms which are done by the religious leaders who preach and encourage the people to love and worship their own God specific to their religion. Atheists exercise their right of freedom of speech to express their view of God and, people are absolutely free to accept or reject it. Indeed they cause no major problem by expressing their thoughts. Whereas preaching or teaching of religious leaders leads to bitter hostilities, conflicts, terrors and wars with all their disastrous and destructive consequences. Well, that was about God what about the other issues such as creation of universe and life that were debated earlier in the book?

*

After the Big Bang, which **heralded the beginning of creation and time**; God created the galaxies and in one of them established unique circumstances for a small planet that we call Earth. Then he created life on this planet and designed the universal evolution for a purpose. There is no reason why life could not also exist in the other planets whether in our galaxy or another one but until we have convincing evidence

335

for such an assumption we have no choice but to assume that life is only on earth. Interestingly, as I was revising and typing these lines, I heard the wonderful news about the landing of Perseverance Rover on Mars; so incredible, so fascinating indeed. The human brain, that amazing machine, has sent this car-sized rover to Mars 220 million Km away from earth and has landed it exactly where it was intended. I was over the moon when I saw the videos and pictures about this historic event. In my heart, I congratulated these genius scientists, I bowed my head to them, took my hat off and admired them but I honestly do not know what words I should use now to express my delight in this astonishing achievement. They want to know if there was life on Mars and there are some signs of life there, I am told. They may prove that billions years ago there was life in Mars and if so most likely the conditions changed and life could no longer continue in that planet; perhaps from freezing cold? And I wondered; probably sometime in future the same will happen on Planet

Earth but this time from burning heat and shortage of water? Sorry, I was taken away with this outstanding success of scientists, now back to my original narrative. I have no doubt that there is a purpose behind all creation and there is a mission for man who unless proved otherwise, is the only of God's creature capable of developing and evolving towards perfection. Of course, the true purpose behind creation will be revealed when man reaches perfection and attains the real knowledge. The belief of Sufi Mystics that, "The cause of creation is absolute beauty; to bring infinite happiness and love is the first creation"; is so fascinating, so close to my heart and indeed offers a truly satisfactory explanation. Man loves anything that is beautiful and if someone claims that he does not love beauty, it is simply because he has not recognised it. Beauty in nature is the reflection of God's quality and it is impossible not to love it. It says in Quran, "Everything is passing away except the face of God." Indeed, everything will pass away except for the essence of beauty and if it was not for

337

that perfect beauty and the ecstasy that one could attain from observing and loving such a quality; there would be no creation. I do believe this is a possible explanation for the cause of creation and precisely based on such assumption I am also convinced about man's mission as I have tried to describe it in this book to the best of my limited understanding.

When Rumi talks about the development, evolution and about dying in one's own false self he says; "From the moment you came into this world a ladder was put in front of you, so that you might ascend and transcend it. From earth (dust) you became plant, from plant you changed to animal and then you became human and you were endowed with intellect and conscience. Behold; the body born of dust how perfect it has become. Why should you fear its end? When were you ever made less by dying?" Indeed, why should we fear of further evolution and ascent on that ladder? Why should we fear dying as animal selves and being reborn as pure humans? How

338

could it ever be a loss?   I firmly believe that evolution is part of God's design and I honestly cannot comprehend, why theists are against evolutionists and the evolutionists deny God.   In fact **universal evolution** is the most important part of **creation**, considering the purpose behind the creation.   I believe that whatever we do; universal evolution as planned by God will continue until that perfect creature emerges from it, which might be the perfect human or totally different creature. But as I've said earlier man has the unique opportunity to reach such perfection, well before that eventuality.

Yes, by definition we are all called humans. But some live more like animals than humans and are wholly under the command of their false selves, fully plunged in their animalistic nature.   These have imprisoned their inner selves and weakened their conscience and perhaps we could refer to them as bad persons and possibly the criminals and perpetrators of atrocities and evil deeds.   Most people improve and partially control the animalistic side of their beings and in this book I have referred to them as good persons. Of course, there are many levels and degrees of being a good person. However, few people continue with their development, evolution and spiritual elevation and truly achieve full control of their false selves and animalistic demands, having freed as well as empowered their real selves; I've called these real humans. Fewer still reach highest level of development and evolution, having virtually annihilated their false selves and become absolutely indifferent and detached from worldly pleasures and those, I have described as perfect humans. Clearly, this is not an agreed–upon classification but it surely helps me to express my understanding of development and indeed of the mission. In the process of evolution from lowest end of such a wide spectrum to its highest level, there are hundreds of steps to take, levels to climb and phases to encounter. In reality, people are scattered within this wide spectrum. Practically and realistically not everyone can be expected to ascend to higher levels and indeed very few could reach the culmination. But surely everyone could take the initial steps towards the self-development, set higher standards in his life and rise above the animal level; showing high moral quality and live nobly. This is the least expected of us and it could be achieved simply by humanistic idealism. In other words, one can develop and partially control animalistic side of one's being in order to become good person, by just believing in moral values and setting up high standards in his personal life, without being religious person and even without belief in God's existence. But I believe having faith or believing and practicing a true religion and more importantly believing in God; smoothes the road leading to final destination and, makes it easier to climb the ladder higher and higher if that is what one intends. So, to be a real human and then to climb further up to become perfect human (which is the core of the mission), one needs a much higher motivation. And it seems to me that, true and uncorrupted religions can provide such a motivation, while monotheism and love of God, would undoubtedly complete that provision. However, I must admit and explain that I have developed mixed feelings and views of religions and faiths.

On the one hand I genuinely believe that corrupted, manipulated and misleading religions as well as faiths comprised of noting but the ceremonies, bizarre rituals and superstitious beliefs; are destructive and indeed obstructive when it comes to our sincere effort for self-improvement and move towards perfection. These types of religions are the cause behind majority of crimes in human history and, the main obstacles for the peace and happiness today. They are also dangerous weapons in the hands of the powerful to create terror, divide the people and rule over them. On the other hand, I believe that all true religions are inseparable in their messages, even though they have been twisted by misunderstandings, ignorance, and superstitions. If the essence of original teaching is taught and if the emphasis is placed on virtues, moral values and humanity then religions are precious vehicles with which one could ascend last difficult steps towards the culmination of his mission and establishing fair and just human societies. In their true uncorrupted form, I see no difference between religions or whichever one accepts and practices. Whenever I reach this point in my thoughts I sincerely hope that one day high-ranking religious leaders would recognize this very fact and, put an end to bitter hostilities amongst religions and their followers. But I know it will remain only a dream for reasons that I have mentioned earlier in the book. Indeed that is not all; when it comes to my confused and controversial feelings and opinion about religions. When I imagine what people without faith or fear of God could do (and examples are not only in history but also at the present time) and when I visualise the situations in such faithless, fearless and Godless societies; then I think, perhaps even the distorted and edited versions of religions are better for

343

human societies than no faith at all. Exactly like imperfect and incomplete laws and orders in communities that are better than no laws and rules at all. If religions, in whatever shape and form make people better persons; then any attempt to weaken their belief is against the interests of humans as a whole. To do justice to the religious leaders, perhaps that is precisely why they do not make any effort to discard corrupted parts of their religions. Perhaps that is why they don't stop people from practicing bizarre ceremonies and faith in superstitions as they don't wish to take any risk and rock the boat. And perhaps this consideration is what lies behind their reluctance to acknowledge that there is only one God and there is no difference in the essence of religions or the messages brought by prophets. And if that is the case then, their inaction is not to protect their own interests and gains and I should not have accused them for that.

However, I do know that one could become a good person by just believing in ethics and humanism but I am afraid this will not work with all people. Besides, this option allows only for limited progress. There cannot be any further development, while false self remains in command. It is my firm conviction that; believing in God's existence, accepting the purpose behind creation and the fact that there is a mission for man to fulfil is enough to develop and move towards perfection and therefore, there is no need for religion. But again, this is not an easy option either, without first reaching a certain level in evolution that requires higher motivation to begin with. Surely the religions in their pure and uncorrupted forms could provide that motivation. In fact it could motivate the traveller to reach a level that religion no longer is needed and, belief in God on its own would be enough for the higher attainments and further ascension towards the summit. I see that I'm displaying a confused mentality about religion. However, I believe once God's existence was genuinely accepted and once he was truly

345

loved then religion becomes least important factor and perhaps could only serve as a device for self-discipline. Even this would be unnecessary all together if one did not need a tool, reminder or stimulator to love and worship God. I'm talking about a love and worship that is exclusively for our own development and evolution, for our own intimate and personal relationships with God and, not a favour to him or expecting any favour from him. This concludes my final convictions about God and religions. But, I confess that my opinion on religions is confusing, which is unsurprising considering their numerous bad and good point. I can hear a reader is shouting at me; get on with it man, do you believe in religion or not? Well, the answer to that; swings more towards no than yes.

*

As for the soul or spirit I believe that the initial gift of God has passed through the genes, generation after the generation and in every human; has become an individual on her own

346

right in a specific physical self or cage as Rumi calls it. When we die, our soul returns and merges with her source which is God, in circumstances that depend on one's state of development. But she does not re-enter into any other body after the death of the original physical self. Clearly, as I do not believe in returning of the same soul to another physical self, I do not believe in any type of incarnation either. I believe each soul dwells in one physical self for only a single lifetime and, that person is accountable for outcome of his worldly life, and the consequences of choices he made with his free will and finally, whether or not he made any attempt to move towards perfection. If one dies prematurely and therefore, does not have enough time to complete the mission, no injustice has been committed in my opinion. This is contrary to those who raise this point for the reason behind their belief in Soule's return to have another chance to develop. I believe God already knows whether they would have made it (or not), had they lived long enough and in favourable situations. So, there is no need to bring the soul back and give her another chance in a different physical self.

I do not believe there are places specifically designed, created and set aside for 'Hell' and 'Heaven'. Jesus Christ had to refer to the kingdom of God and Prophet Mohammad had to refer to charming gardens in order to illustrate the beauty of life after death, if man evolved and successfully moved towards perfection in his life on earth. In the mind of people Heaven has always been manifested in the image of things on earth such as garden or kingdom and God in the image of man. I can understand this, but I believe the teaching of Zoroaster that Heaven is the best state of mind and Hell is the worst is an excellent starter for a realistic contemplation about those places. And in that sense; we experience Heaven or Hell while living in this world. In my view, after physical death if the owner of body (or cage) had progressed in his worldly life and moved towards perfection; the soul would be in absolute peace and ultimate bliss, while returning to God and merging with source, where she will be conscious of being in God's presence and mindful of being part of him. She will see perfect beauty, feel absolute peace and enjoy infinite bliss forever, and that is the Heaven. But if the person had continued living in the animalistic side of his being and had fallen into hedonistic life with no effort in development and move towards the perfection; he will not have those privileges. She too will return to God but she will not be conscious of being part of him or have any feeling of perfect peace and true happiness, and that is Hell. Even before physical death, if one develops and becomes a real human, he will see the beauty of being in such a status and therefore will live in full satisfaction, pride and peace. And in that case one will be in best state of mind or Heaven as Zoroaster said. On the other hand if the person lives in his false self, immersed in materialistic world may feel and see the ugliness and disgrace of living like an animal and will certainly experience the essence of being in Hell in his worldly life, if he has not killed his conscience altogether. As for a Judgement Day, I am unable to comprehend its necessity when God already knows who deserves to live in infinite happiness and who deserves to suffer the cost of his affairs and live in infinite misery. But if for reasons unknown to man; Judgement day is in God's plan then, all I can say is that yes, it is indeed in the power of God to do so. With that statement, the narration of the journey ends here and I close this book with clarification of few points and also sharing with you my dreams and hopes. Obviously the problems that human societies are facing today are not just consequences of having different religions or hostilities and conflicts created amongst followers. Practically and realistically educational, cultural, social, political and issues related to economics are much stronger factors in creating these unfortunate conditions that human finds himself deeply affected by and trapped within. I've not touched upon anyone of these factors as my aim was only to narrate a spiritual journey (alongside just a summary of political events that I thought influenced the path of my journey). However, in previous pages I have repeatedly referred to my hopes and dreams of what religious and political leaders could do to put an end to all the hatred, hostility, conflict and war, arising from different religions. But I've also added that most likely such hope will always remain as dream, because those in power would never put their own interests in peril. I have said they will continue using religions and God to create terrors and wars so that they could maintain their power and continue with their affluent and luxurious lives. Such a harsh opinion and verdict about leaders (whether religious or secular) is definitely accurate for some but not for all. I now realise such generalisation is incorrect and by no means justified. In reality many of these victims of my unfair judgement may genuinely wish and even try to end the hostilities and solve such problems but having failed to make a real progress, they conclude that, such a task is almost impossible as wounds are too deep and chronic to heal, divisions or knots are too complex to untie and hostilities and hatreds are too old to reconcile. However, today with partly fruitful examples of peace and reconciliations in Europe and Africa perhaps my conclusion is rather pessimistic. Perhaps hope for wider achievement in forgiveness, reconciliation and peace is more realistic. There is still some hope that leaders and those in power would stop confining all the blessing, whether temporal or eternal, to themselves and their own people. It seems likely that the dreams and predictions such as: "If man finds his real self and lives by his true nature, which is higher than physical urges and social pressures, there is a hope to save civilisation from ruin", could materialise in reality. Indeed, man has come a long way in his development and evolution (considering the ignorance and barbarisms of our ancestors and their shameful crimes and atrocities) and such improvement will continue, I hope. I don't mean that we no longer see barbarism and atrocities of course we do, but not as much the past. We definitely see all sorts of crimes being committed, by individuals or gangs and more often by super powers with new excuses, deceiving slogans and modern technologies.   But today more and more people are speaking out against such inhumane behaviours and there is a real hope that in future the crime and destruction that we have seen in recent decades, will decrease and even cease to exist.

There is some hope that; today's young individuals who would be tomorrow's scientists, thinkers and religious or political leaders would progress further and as good people or better still as real humans, pave the way for future generations so that, they may achieve much higher levels in evolution and move towards perfection faster.   Universal, natural and personal evolution side by side will surly continue and the remnants of human's animalistic nature will get thinner and weaker, while humanistic side of his being will get stronger and stronger, purer and purer; generation after generation.   There will be a time when everyone is after further development and races towards perfection by being at the service of others (without expecting reward in return), by being involved in charities (without any attempt to show off) and by eagerly helping the people in need. Indeed, in the near future there will be a shortage of people in need that one passionately wishes to reach and help. There will be no poverty, no hunger, no discrimination, no inequality, no racism, no oppression, no atrocity nor any injustice in human societies. There will be no bitterness, no hostility, no hatred, no war or destruction. It will be all brotherhood, sisterhood, peace and happiness. What a wonderful world it would be, what a beautiful dream it is. I wish I could say that these are not just wishful dreams and one day they will come true. Direction of evolution is towards the perfection, man cannot go backwards; he will get there. Human beings will see and admire perfect beauty, feel pure love, experience absolute peace and live in infinite felicity. I wish I could say that today's children, tomorrow's young men and women and future generations will work much harder and better than we tried and far more than our ancestors did; to make theses dreams a reality.

The end

In Searching God

Other publications of the author:

1-Peoples' Servant and Resemblance

2-Agony of Deniz

3-Intellectuals of Café Naderi (This is now out of print and
In Searching God is the revised version of it).

In Searching God